JOHANN SEBASTIAN BACH

# St John Passion

JOHANN SEBASTIAN BACH

# St John Passion

## Genesis, Transmission, and Meaning

ALFRED DÜRR

Translated by

ALFRED CLAYTON

UNIVERSITY PRESS

**OXFORD**
UNIVERSITY PRESS

Great Clarendon Street, Oxford, OX2 6DP
Oxford University Press is a department of the University of Oxford.
It furthers the University's objective of excellence in research, scholarship,
and education by publishing worldwide in

Oxford New York

Athens Auckland Bangkok Bogotá Buenos Aires Calcutta
Cape Town Chennai Dar es Salaam Delhi Florence Hong Kong Istanbul
Karachi Kuala Lumpur Madrid Melbourne Mexico City Mumbai
Nairobi Paris São Paulo Shanghai Singapore Taipei Tokyo Toronto Warsaw

and associated companies in Berlin Ibadan

Oxford is a registered trade mark of Oxford University Press
in the UK and certain other countries

Published in the United States
by Oxford University Press Inc., New York



First published 2000



British Library Cataloguing in Publication Data
Data available

Library of Congress Cataloging in Publication Data

Dürr, Alfred, 1918–
[Johannes-Passion von Johann Sebastian Bach. English]
Johann Sebastian Bach's St. John Passion : genesis, transmission,
and meaning / Alfred Dürr ; translated by Alfred Clayton.
p. cm.
Includes bibliographical references and index.
1. Bach, Johann Sebastian, 1685–1750. Johannespassion.
I. Title.
ML410.B13D813 1999 782.23—dc21 99–32937

ISBN 0-19-816240-5

1 3 5 7 9 10 8 6 4 2

Typeset by Regent Typesetting, London
Printed in Great Britain
on acid-free paper by
Biddles Ltd., Guildford and King's Lynn

# CONTENTS

# PREFACE

The purpose of this book is to acquaint scholars and ordinary listeners in a comprehensible manner with the problems associated with Bach's St John Passion, which in part are rather complicated. However, in addition to providing an introduction to the work itself, the primary aim of this study, there is a fairly detailed description of the way in which the sources have been transmitted. This requires some justification.

The American musicologist Arthur Mendel was the first scholar to study the original sources of the St John Passion, which constitute one of the most thorny problems of Bach scholarship, with the tools provided by modern textual criticism. In 1974 he published the results of his investigations in the *Kritischer Bericht* of the *Neue Bach-Ausgabe*. Yet his research was not primarily based on the new insights provided by general research into the chronology of Bach's works.[1] Rather, it was founded on the internal evidence of the sources themselves. For this reason Mendel's findings are particularly compelling, especially in view of the fact that they were made at a time when the new chronology had not become generally accepted.[2] The vindicatory nature of Mendel's arguments and his attempts to dispose of any possible objections forthwith lead to a painstaking and exhaustive presentation of the facts that makes it rather difficult for the ordinary reader to see them in perspective.[3] Now that the results of Mendel's research and the new chronology are no longer in dispute, the facts can be presented rather more succinctly. It is to be hoped that this will make the subject accessible to a much wider readership, and, in the final analysis, obtain for Mendel's important work the recognition it deserves.

The elucidation of the meaning of the work tries to strike a compromise between analysis, which can easily become too detailed, and the mere demonstration of general relationships, which can easily become rather superficial. For this reason a number of representative move-

[1] Dürr, *Chr*[2]; *TBSt* 4/5.

[2] See Friedrich Smend, 'Was bleibt? Zu Friedrich Blumes Bach-Bild', *Der Kirchenmusiker*, 13 (1962), 178–88.

[3] Thus even those who profess to be scholars sometimes ignore Mendel's work. See *BJ* (1986), p. 146.

ments have been analysed in greater detail. With regard to the rest of the Passion, an attempt is made to describe in brief the characteristic features of each piece. The aim of these remarks is to draw the listener's attention to what is heard, and thus to enable him to understand the musical work as it unfolds in time.

In view of this some readers may regret the fact that one of the favourite topics of modern commentators, namely number symbolism, and other cryptic ciphers that are merely speculative, including those of a theological nature, receive scant attention, if indeed they are mentioned at all. Although Bach's music undoubtedly contains certain obvious kinds of number symbolism (and they are obvious because they are audible—for example, in the B minor Mass the duet is a symbol of the second person of the Trinity), the true extent of such influences on the music (especially when they are incapable of being perceived) remains questionable. Without wishing to come down in favour of a purely positivist approach, the present study adheres to the premiss that what Bach had to say to his listeners in church was meant to be heard and that it was not intended to be a secret message destined for future generations.

Ideally, the reader should have access to a score or at least a vocal score of the work. The text of the St John Passion has been included (see below, pp. 134–77) in order to enable the reader to compare it with the versions of the text by Brockes and others (reproduced on pp. 42–8) that served as models for the poet who wrote it.

The author owes a debt of gratitude to all those who contributed to the completion of this book: the State Library in Berlin (SBB, also for permission to reproduce the illustrations), Elke Axmacher, and the editorial assistant, Ruth Blume. He is also indebted to the participants who attended the seminar at the Internationale Bachakademie Stuttgart in March 1986, in particular to Werner Breig, Peter Kreyssig, Martin Petzoldt, and Meinrad Walter. In Göttingen Yoshitake Kobayashi provided invaluable advice on the sources.

Alfred Dürr

Bovenden, October 1987

# ACKNOWLEDGEMENT

The translation of this work was supported by a grant from Inter Nationes, Bonn, Germany.

# ABBREVIATIONS

| | |
|---|---|
| A | Alto |
| B | Bass |
| b./bb. | bar/bars (followed by bar numbers) |
| bc | basso continuo |
| BG | Bach-Gesellschaft (Complete Edition) (Leipzig, 1851–99) |
| *BJ* | *Bach-Jahrbuch* |
| Breig (1985) | Werner Breig, 'Zu den Turba-Chören von Bachs Johannes-Passion', *Geistliche Musik: Studien zu ihrer Geschichte und Funktion im 18. und 19. Jahrhundert* (*Hamburger Jahrbuch für Musikwissenschaft*, 8; Laaber, 1985), 65–96 |
| BWV | Wolfgang Schmieder, *Thematisch-systematisches Verzeichnis der musikalischen Werke von Johann Sebastian Bach: Bach-Werke-Verzeichnis* (Wiesbaden, 1990) |
| Cemb. | Cembalo |
| Chafe (1981) | Eric Chafe, 'Key Structure and Tonal Allegory in the Passions of J. S. Bach: An Introduction', *Current Musicology*, 31 (1981), 39–54 |
| Chafe (1982) | Eric Chafe, 'J. S. Bach's St. Matthew Passion: Aspects of Planning, Structure, and Chronology', *Journal of the American Musicological Society*, 35 (1982), 49–114 |
| Chafe (1988) | Eric Chafe, 'Bach's St. John Passion: Theology and Musical Structure', in Don O. Franklin (ed.), *New Bach Studies* (Cambridge, 1988) |
| Crit. Report | Critical Report |
| *Dok* i, ii, iii | *Bach-Dokumente*, ed. Bach-Archiv Leipzig, *Schriftstücke von der Hand Johann Sebastian Bachs*, ed. and with commentary by Werner Neumann and Hans-Joachim Schulze (Kassel and Leipzig, 1963); ii. *Fremdschriftliche und gedruckte Dokumente zur* |

| | |
|---|---|
| | *Lebensgeschichte Johann Sebastian Bachs 1685–1750*, ed. and with commentary by Werner Neumann and Hans-Joachim Schulze (Kassel and Leipzig, 1969); iii. *Dokumente zum Nachwirken Johann Sebastian Bachs 1750–1800*, ed. and with commentary by Hans-Joachim Schulze (Kassel and Leipzig, 1972) |
| Dürr, *Chr*$^2$ | Alfred Dürr, *Zur Chronologie der Vokalwerke J. S. Bachs*, 2nd edn., repr. of *BJ* 1957 edn. with notes and addenda |
| ed. | editor, edited by |
| edn. | edition |
| EG | Evangelisches Gesangbuch |
| fo. | folio |
| fltr | flauto traverso |
| harps | harpsichord |
| *HHA* | Hallische Händel-Ausgabe (complete edn.), ed. Georg-Friedrich-Händel-Gesellschaft (Kassel and Leipzig, 1955– ) |
| instr | instrument(s) |
| Mendel, *KB* | Johann Sebastian Bach, *Neue Ausgabe sämtlicher Werke*, ser. II, vol. 4. *Johannes-Passion. Kritischer Bericht von Arthur Mendel* (Kassel and Leipzig, 1974) |
| Mendel, I | Arthur Mendel, 'Traces of the Pre-History of Bach's St. John and St. Matthew Passions', in *Festschrift Otto Erich Deutsch zum 80. Geburtstag* (Kassel, 1963), 31–48 |
| Mendel, II | Arthur Mendel, 'More on the Weimar Origin of Bach's *O Mensch, bewein* (BWV 244/35)', *Journal of the American Musicological Society*, 17 (1964), 203–6 |
| *Mf* | *Die Musikforschung* (1948– ) |
| *MGG* | *Die Musik in Geschichte und Gegenwart*, 17 vols. (Kassel, 1949–79, 1986) |
| MS, MSS | manuscript, manuscripts |
| n. | note, footnote |
| *NBA* | Johann Sebastian Bach, *Neue ausgabe sämtlicher Werke. Neue Bach-Ausgabe* (Kassel and Leipzig, 1954– ). In the present book NBA on its own always refers to the edn. of the St John Passion, ser. II, vol. 4, and to the identical miniature score (Bärenreiter TP 197) |

| | |
|---|---|
| ob | oboe |
| ob da c | oboe da caccia |
| ob d'am | oboe d'amore |
| obb | obbligato |
| org | organo (organ) |
| S | Soprano |
| SBB | Staatsbibliothek zu Berlin, Preußischer Kulturbesitz |
| Schering, *KM* | Arnold Schering, *Johann Sebastian Bachs Leipziger Kirchenmusik: Studien und Wege zu ihrer Erkenntnis* (Leipzig, 1936) |
| Schering, *L* | Arnold Schering, *Johann Sebastian Bach und das Musikleben Leipzigs im 18. Jahrhundert* (Musikgeschichte Leipzigs, 3; Leipzig, 1941) |
| Schulze, *St* | Hans-Joachim Schulze, *Studien zur Bach-Überlieferung im 18. Jahrhundert* (Leipzig, 1984) |
| Smend (1926) | Friedrich Smend, 'Die Johannes-Passion von Bach. Auf ihren Bau untersucht', *BJ* (1926), 105–28; repr. in id., *Bach-Studien: Gesammelte Reden und Aufsätze*, ed. Christoph Wolff (Kassel, 1969), 11–23 |
| Smend (1947) | Friedrich Smend, 'Luther und Bach', *Der Anfang*, 2 (Berlin, 1947); repr. in id., *Bach-Studien*, 153–75 |
| Smend (1951) | Friedrich Smend, *Bach in Köthen* (Berlin, 1951) [Eng. trans. 1985] |
| Spitta | Philipp Spitta, *Johann Sebastian Bach*, i (Leipzig, 1873), ii (Leipzig, 1880) [Eng. trans. (1884–99)] |
| str | strings, here always violin I, II, and viola; continuo string parts are subsumed under the abbreviation bc. |
| T | Tenor |
| *TBSt* 1, 2/3, 4/5, 6 | *Tübinger Bach-Studien*, ed. Walter Gerstenberg,<br>1: Georg von Dadelsen, *Bemerkungen zur Handschrift Johann Sebastian Bachs, seiner Famille und seines Kreises* (Trossingen, 1957)<br>2/3: Paul Kast, *Die Bach-Handschriften der Berliner Staatsbibliothek* (Trossingen, 1958)<br>4/5: Georg von Dadelsen, *Beiträge zur Chronologie der Werke Johann Sebastian Bachs* (Trossingen, 1958)<br>6: Doris Finke-Hecklinger, *Tanzcharaktere in Johann Sebastian Bachs Vokalmusik* (Trossingen, 1970) |

| | |
|---|---|
| va | viola |
| va da g | viola da gamba |
| va d'am | viola d'amore |
| vn | violin |
| vol. | volume |
| Weiß | Wisso Weiß, *Katalog der Wasserzeichen in Bachs Originalhandschriften unter musikwissenschaftlicher Mitarbeit von Yoshitake Kobayashi* (Johann Sebastian Bach, *Neue Ausgabe sämtlicher Werke*, ser. IX, vol. 1; Kassel and Leipzig, 1985) |
| WM | watermark |
| ww | woodwinds (in the St John Passion; flauto traverso I, II, oboe I, II, also oboe d'amore or oboe da caccia I, II) |
| Zahn | Johannes Zahn, *Die Melodien der deutschen evangelischen Kirchenlieder*, i–vi (Gütersloh, 1889; repr. Hildesheim, 1963) |

If their names are not known, the scribes of the original parts of the St John Passion are referred to as in Dürr, *Chr*², pp. 147 ff.

# I

# Genesis

The attempt to reconstruct the genesis of Bach's St John Passion on the basis of the extant and unfortunately incomplete manuscript sources resembles the work of an archaeologist faced with the task of piecing together an antique vase from innumerable small fragments of pottery. At the beginning there exists merely a vague idea of what the vessel that he wishes to reconstruct may have looked like. It is only as a result of a great deal of trial and error that the work finally reaches a state the beholder finds convincing. This, and only this, he will exclaim, is what it must have looked like.

In the case of the St John Passion the minute 'archaeological' work has been done by Mendel, *KB*. Thus we can circumvent a detailed account of the process of reconstruction and present the result as seen by modern scholarship. The evidence for this is stated in Chapter II, which deals with transmission. It also provides an opportunity to discuss the differing scholarly interpretations of the sources.

Of course, the incomplete nature of the transmitted sources means that there are gaps in our knowledge when we attempt to reconstruct the genesis of the work. Here again a musicologist is in the same position as an archaeologist who is forced either to leave out missing fragments of his vase or to supply them on a hypothetical basis. A conscientious scholar will always point out the doubtful character of such substitutions.

## INTRODUCTION: DID BACH COMPOSE A PASSION BEFORE 1724?

As we shall see, the first documented performance of Bach's St John Passion took place on Good Friday, 1724. However, only some of the parts have survived from this performance, and no score. The question thus arises of whether this really was the first performance, or whether other performances preceded it.

There is in fact only negative proof for the assumption that the work was first performed in 1724, though I believe it to be convincing. For a start, Philipp Spitta's assertion (ii. 348, 813–14 [Eng. trans. ii. 519, 710–11]) that Bach had already written out the first set of parts for the St John Passion in Cöthen is merely the result of his confusing similar watermarks, a pardonable error in view of when he was writing.[1] In fact no Cöthen manuscript of the Passion has survived, and there is not the slightest indication that such a manuscript ever existed. Furthermore, a Passion was certainly performed in Leipzig at St Thomas's Church on Good Friday 1723 while the post of cantor was vacant.[2] Yet there is no evidence whatsoever that this was directed by Bach, as Bernhard Friedrich Richter deduced from the information supplied by Spitta. In fact, if Bach had directed this performance of a Passion, it may safely be assumed that, in some way or other, it would have been mentioned in the Council Minutes relating to his election to the post of cantor at St Thomas's on 22 April 1723 (four weeks after Good Friday!).[3] Finally, even if, contrary to all the evidence, Bach performed a Passion at St Thomas's Church on Good Friday 1723, it can hardly have been the St John Passion, which would thus have been played for three years in succession in the Leipzig *Hauptkirchen* (principal churches). In any case, it is certainly odd that it was performed again in 1725 (Bach must have had reasons of which we are unaware). A third performance a year earlier would have been too much of a sign of creative poverty. Bach's biography provides no evidence for a similar occurrence, not even one that resembles it approximately.

This consideration prompts us to ask whether Bach—even if it was not in 1723—had actually written another Passion before 1724.[4] In fact only two of his five Passions[5] have survived (BWV 244–5). The loss of a third is documented (BWV 247), whereas nothing is known about the other two. Again, early on in the Weimar period Bach copied out (or had copied out) the parts of a St Mark Passion by Reinhard Keiser.[6] So

[1] Weiß, 28 (used by Bach in 1721 and 1722) and 29 (used by Bach in 1724 and 1725). See Ch. II for further details.

[2] Bernhard Friedrich Richter, 'Zur Geschichte der Passionsaufführungen in Leipzig', *BJ* (1911), 50–9; *Dok.* ii, no. 180, pp. 140–2.

[3] See *Dok.* ii, no. 129, pp. 93–5.

[4] See Alfred Dürr, 'Zu den verschollenen Passionen Bachs', *BJ* (1949–50), 81–99, and Mendel, I, II.

[5] According to the 'Obituary'. See *Dok.* iii, no. 666, pp. 80–93: at p. 86.

[6] See Andreas Glöckner, 'Johann Sebastian Bachs Aufführungen zeitgenössischer Passionsmusiken', *BJ* (1977), 75–119: at 76–89. The copying of parts always suggests a performance (at least a prospective one), whereas a manuscript copy of a score may simply have been a collector's item.

why should he not have composed and performed a Passion of his own in Weimar? A reference by Hilgenfeldt to a passion of 1717 would sound fairly unconvincing[7] if Version II of the St John Passion did not contain a number of movements that could well have come from an earlier passion by Bach. (On the subject of Version II, see Ch. 1. 2.)

Recent research has shown that Bach was in Gotha around the time of Good Friday, 1717.[8] Bach's first (?) Passion may well have been written at this time, and some or all of the movements in Version II of the St John Passion referred to above may have formed part of this work. However, it is unlikely that Bach composed a Passion during his years at Cöthen (1717–22), and it is highly improbable that he composed one for Leipzig in 1723.

## 1. VERSION I (1724)

In order to make it easier to compare the various versions, the starting-point for the following remarks will be the one on which the normal printed editions and in particular the main section of *NBA* II/4 (together with the corresponding miniature score) are based. It provides the background for a description of the deviations peculiar to each of the different versions. Lack of space means that I cannot include a list of variants which aims to be as complete as possible, as in Mendel, *KB*.

As we shall see in Chapter II, the first version of the St John Passion can only be partially reconstructed on the basis of some of the parts (the ripieno parts of the chorus, violin I and II, and continuo), and to some extent, from movement 10, bar $42^b$ onwards, from the readings of the surviving original score A. However, a series of questions remains unanswered, in particular with regard to the participation of woodwinds. The reason for this is not only the loss of the relevant parts, but also the frequently imprecise instrumental indications in the score. As we shall see, the parts of the solo voices have also survived incomplete, particularly in the case of movement 33.

Of course, by and large Version I corresponds to the familiar final version, though there are a number of minor differences. The most important ones are as follows:

[7] Carl Ludwig Hilgenfeldt, *Johann Sebastian Bach's Leben, Wirken und Werke* (Leipzig, 1850, repr. Hilversum, 1965), 114: 'Bach is said to have composed one of the other three [passions] in 1717'.

[8] See Eva-Maria Ranft, 'Ein unbekannter Aufenthalt Johann Sebastian Bachs in Gotha?', *BJ* (1985), 165–6, and Andreas Glöckner, 'Neue Spuren zu Bachs "Weimarer" Passion', in *Bericht über die Wissenschaftliche Konferenz anläßlich des 69. Bach-Festes der Neuen Bachgesellschaft, Leipzig, 29. und 30. März 1994* (Hildesheim, 1995), 33–46.

(a) The style is occasionally less elaborate. It is not as yet enlivened by embellishments or notes that fill intervals, etc. For movements 1 to 10, first readings, inasmuch as they can be ascertained, are given in appendix I of the *NBA*, pp. 167–205.

(b) The extent to which transverse flutes participate in the work continues to be an open question. In the original score A the heading, which was written about 1739, still fails to mention transverse flutes, although Version II of 1725 already has flauto traverso parts. Did Bach originally conceive the Passion without transverse flutes? Or did a versatile musician, who normally played a different instrument, have to step in to play the transverse flute in certain movements? The problem remains unresolved, and the reader is referred to Appendix I for a more detailed discussion of this issues involved.

(c) In Version I, movement 33 comprised only 3 bars (I refer to this version as movement $33^{I}$). As the original score already has the lengthier reading of Versions II and IV at this point, and as the solo tenor part, like most of the other parts of Version I, is no longer extant, only the surviving continuo part affords evidence of this short version. It is discussed in greater detail in Appendix II. If my view of the matter is correct (it is based on Mendel, *KB*), then in Version I only the first of the two passages of text interpolated into St John's account of the Passion was taken from St Matthew (movement $12^{c}$, Matt. 26: 75), whereas the second passage, movement $33^{I}$, was based on Mark 15: 38.

### 2. VERSION II (1725)

This version has survived in a form that is virtually complete. The only missing items are the parts for transverse flutes, oboes, and viola in movement $1^{II}$, 'O Mensch, bewein dein Sünde groß', which in Version III were replaced by the corresponding parts for 'Herr, unser Herrscher'. However, it is possible to reconstruct them with the help of the sources of the St Matthew Passion (1736).

As we have seen, the reason why Bach performed the St John Passion in two consecutive years remains something of a mystery, and none of the attempts to shed light on the matter have come up with a hard-and-fast answer. For a more detailed discussion of this problem see Appendix III.

It seems that, only a year later, Bach himself no longer wished to perform the same version of the Passion. This is demonstrated by the changes he now introduced:

Movement 1 was replaced by $1^{II}$, 'O Mensch, bewein dein Sünde groß'.

Movement $11^{+}$, 'Himmel reiße, Welt erbebe' was newly inserted after movement 11.

Movement 13 was replaced by $13^{II}$, 'Zerschmettert mich, ihr Felsen und ihr Hügel'.

Movements 19–20 were replaced by $19^{II}$, 'Ach windet euch nicht so, geplagte Seelen'.

Movement $33^{I}$ was replaced by the seven-bar movement 33 that we know today.

Movement 40 was replaced by $40^{II}$, 'Christe, du Lamm Gottes'.

Of these movements, 33 was without doubt newly composed in order to replace the text of Mark 15: 38 with that of Matthew 27: 51–2, which corresponded more closely to the words of the following arioso (movement 34).

The provenance of the other movements can only be surmised (see the literature referred to in n. 4, above). 'O Mensch, bewein dein Sünde groß' (movement $1^{II}$) was probably based on an original version in D major,[9] and this may well have been written in Bach's Weimar period, in which case the choir pitch (*Chorton*) would have been D major, whereas the recorders and oboes would have played in chamber pitch (*Kammerton*), F major. However, the Weimar origins of the movement do not seem to have been conclusively established. Mendel's main argument in favour of such origins, the intervallic emendations in the woodwind staves of the autograph manuscript of the St Matthew Passion, does not in fact settle the matter (see Crit. Report, *NBA*, II/5, p. 80). In the case of the St Matthew Passion (1736) it is perfectly possible to trace the work back to an original in D major. However, although this also seems probable in the case of the St John Passion (1725), as Mendel has demonstrated with reference to certain voice-leading peculiarities, conclusive proof is lacking, so that in addition to the most obvious relationship:

Weimar (?) D major
1725 E♭ major
1736 E major

it is not entirely possible to rule out the following:

1725 E♭ major
c.1726/1735 D major
1736 E major.

[9] See Mendel, I, II, and the Crit. Report, *NBA* II/5, p. 80.

Furthermore, the dimensions of the chorale chorus are unusually large if we assume that it was written in Weimar, though not inconceivable for the time around 1716/17 (see above, Hilgenfeldt, n. 7, and Glöckner, n. 6).

'Himmel reiße, Welt erbebe' (movement $11^{+}$) was probably written before 1725, presumably in Bach's Weimar period. This becomes especially apparent in the cantus firmus version of the sixth line of the chorale 'Jesu Leiden, Pein und Tod'. It is improbable that in 1725 Bach would have departed so radically from the form of the melody selected a year earlier for movements 14, 28, and 32 if he had not been prompted to do so by an earlier version:

There is no indication that 'Zerschmettert mich' (movement $13^{II}$) and 'Ach windet euch nicht so' (movement $19^{II}$) were written before 1725. However, it is possible to come to conclusions similar to those reached in the case of movements $1^{II}$ (?), $11^{+}$, and $40^{II}$.

At any rate, 'Christe, du Lamm Gottes' (movement $40^{II}$) had been used before Good Friday 1725 as the final chorale of Cantata No. 23, 'Du wahrer Gott und Davids Sohn'.[10] There is no conclusive evidence to suggest that the movement had been written at an even earlier date.

It has frequently been surmised that the replacement of the introductory chorus (movement 1) with a chorale chorus ($1^{II}$), the insertion of an aria with chorale ($11^{+}$), and the much more elaborate treatment of the final chorale ($40^{II}$) should be seen in the context of the 1724–5 cycle of chorale cantatas.[11] There is no doubt an element of truth in this. However, it should be remembered that the chorale cantata, at least in the context of the Leipzig tradition,[12] had a different function, namely to complement the chorale sermon. There was of course no place for such a function in the context of Good Friday evensong. Furthermore, the

[10] Until the Crit. Report *NBA* 1/8 is published see Christoph Wolff, 'Bachs Leipziger Kantoratsprobe und die Aufführungsgeschichte der Kantate "Du wahrer Gott und Davids Sohn", BWV 23', *BJ* (1978), 78–94.

[11] See e.g. Wolff (cited above, n. 2), 88 and Chafe (1982: 110).

[12] See Alfred Dürr, 'Zur Entstehungsgeschichte des Bachschen Choralkantaten-Jahrgangs', in Martin Geck (ed.), *Bach-Interpretationen* (Göttingen, 1969), 7–11.

excision of these movements in the subsequent versions would remain inexplicable. After all, the chorale cantatas were later performed in their original states. Whether there is any truth to this theory must remain a matter for debate. However, Bach's alterations may simply have been due to a desire to make some changes to a Passion that had to be performed two years in succession.

Evidently Bach did not consider Version II of the St John Passion to be a step on the path leading to a final version, for most of the 'improvements' were removed when the work was next performed. One of the reasons for this may have been that he wished to perform the hypothetical earlier work (or works) from which he had borrowed some of the movements, and that he was unwilling to incorporate the latter permanently in the St John Passion. In order to understand this procedure correctly, we must attempt to develop a more profound understanding of the mentality of a composer of the age of Bach, who would have been wholly familiar with the concept of the 'pasticcio' (pastry), which involved assembling a multi-movement work from compositions of diverse origin and even by different composers. The favourite genre in this regard was opera. However, the music of a Passion was not infrequently put together in this manner, and the idea of intellectual property rarely became an issue. Thus when Bach occasionally had recourse to movements taken from his own compositions, this was certainly not unusual. In particular, it usually had nothing to do with the notion that the movement concerned was not suited to its original location and had at last found its true vocation. The suitability for a performance alone determined the selection of the pieces, not the concept of an ideal and immortal work of art.

## 3. VERSION III (C.1730)

This version, which is difficult to date precisely, is characterized by two features: the removal of the changes made in Version II and the excision of the passages from St Matthew's Gospel. Thus movements 1 and 19–20 returned to their original positions. Movement $11^{+}$ was omitted, and so, for reasons that are difficult to understand, was the final chorale (movements 40 and $40^{II}$).

It is not quite clear why Bach discarded the inserts from St Matthew. The most plausible reason may have been an injunction from the church authorities (for details see App. III, p. 120). If Bach himself agreed to the excision of these passages, it would be difficult to account for the fact that he reversed his decision in Version IV.

As a result of this alteration to the text of the Gospel it also became necessary to make changes in the movements that commented on the biblical text. Thus, if we disregard a few minor deviations, the structure of Version III was as follows:

Movements 1–$12^{b}$ as in Version I.
Movement $12^{c}$ only to b. $31^{a}$, with a cadence in B minor.
Movement $13^{III}$, an aria that is no longer extant, inserted as a replacement for 13 or $13^{II}$.
Movement 14 in G major instead of A major.
Movements 15–32 as in Version I.
Movement $33^{III}$, evidently a 'Sinfonia' that is no longer extant, inserted as a replacement for movements 33–5.
Movements 36–9 as in Version I.

Movement $13^{III}$ must have been a tenor aria with string accompaniment and continuo (and without woodwinds) in a key that fitted in with the B minor of movement $12^{c}$—at the same time making it necessary to transpose movement 14 from A major to G major (beginning in E minor instead of F♯ minor)—in other words, probably in E minor or G major. Since neither the aria 'Ach, mein Sinn' (movement 13) nor 'Zerschmettert mich' (movement $13^{II}$) would have required this transposition, it must have been a completely different piece. It is impossible to say anything else about this movement.

Movement $33^{III}$ is even more mysterious. Apparently the entries in the parts have always been incomplete. However, the movement seems to have been a 'Sinfonia', and it is fairly certain that it was at least for violin I and continuo. There is (now) no reference whatsoever to the piece in the woodwind, violin II, and viola parts. Of course, inserts may well have existed, though the NB indication that is usually present in such cases is missing. That a sinfonia in fact filled in the gap between movements 32 and 36 can primarily be deduced from the fact that, whereas Bach's copyists occasionally omitted an indication (in this case 'Sinfonia tacet' or even 'Sinfonia vide sub Signo . . .') in some of the parts, they were not given to including references to a non-existent movement in the others.

Some of the changes in the scoring of this version were probably makeshift arrangements that became necessary on account of missing instruments or players. They cannot be interpreted as a change of taste on the part of Bach. This is particularly true in the case of the violas d'amore in movements 19 and 20, which were replaced by solo violins with mutes, and in that of the lute in movement 19, which was replaced by obbligato organ.

## 4. VERSION IV (C.1749)

The evidence of the composer's own handwriting suggests that this latest version, which is transmitted in original parts, can only come from the last years of Bach's life.

It is characterized by the restoration of the inserts from St Matthew's Gospel with all that this entails, including the final chorale (movement 40); by the accrual of a number of additional performing parts; and by certain textual alterations in movements based on free poetry.

Thus Bach to all intents and purposes returns to Version I. Only movement 33 is retained in the enlarged state of Version II (i.e. the text comes from St Matthew and not from St Mark). With regard to the increase in the number of performing parts, the possibility can of course not be wholly excluded that in the process some of the older parts were discarded. However, it is far more likely that Bach envisaged an enlargement of the instrumental forces employed. Hence the following were added to the forces previously required:

1 desk violin I
1 desk viola
1 desk continuo
1 harpsichord (perhaps Bach had hitherto played from the score)

One of the existing continuo parts was arranged 'pro Bassono grosso', i.e. for double bassoon (although the interpretation 'for ripieno bassoon' cannot altogether be ruled out)[13]. It remains unclear which instrument was intended to replace the original lute part in movement 19. Bach seems to have vacillated between the harpsichord (a part was newly written out for Version IV) and the organ (a late autograph addition to the organ part of Version III states: 'To be played on the organ with 8' and 4' Gedackt'), though his final preference never became clearly apparent. However, as in Version III, he had to find a makeshift replacement for the missing lute.

[13] In a concerto for recorder, viola da gamba, and strings by Georg Philipp Telemann (Darmstadt, Mus. 1033/59), the term 'Violino grosso' is used for ripieno violins I and II. I am indebted to Klaus Hofmann (Göttingen) for this information.

The textual changes, which will be examined in greater detail when discussing the text (Ch. III.2.d), and which are reproduced on pp. 174–7, initially concern movements 9, 19, and 20. Further textual changes (in movement 39) were probably only made after Bach's death, though it is possible to trace the idea back to Version IV.

A common feature of these textual revisions is their striving for greater rationality. Much of the pictorial quality of the original text, which Bach reproduced with the help of musical figures, is jettisoned, and the congruity of text and music suffers as a result. It is therefore questionable whether Bach himself was prompted to make these changes, or whether he was forced to make them on account of an injunction from the church authorities.

## 5. SCORE A

In view of its complex origins it is not possible to classify the original score A as a separate 'version'.

Towards the end of the 1730s Bach began to replace the original score of the St John Passion, which we will call X, with a new copy, A. On fo. 10 this autograph section A ends in the middle of movement 10 (b. 42[a], Evangelist, tenth semiquaver; continuo, third crotchet). The score must have remained in this state until Bach, in the last years of his life, had it completed by a copyist in conjunction with the preparation of the parts for Version IV.

Thus Score A consists of two heterogeneous sections. The autograph beginning is to all intents and purposes based on Versions I = IV, though there are numerous differences which show that the composer was intent on making certain improvements. A general overview is provided by the *NBA*, which prints two versions of movements 1 to 10: appendix 1 in principle reproduces Version I, whereas the main text reproduces the version of score A. However, the reader is referred to Mendel, *KB*, which contains more detailed information.

As far as can be ascertained, the rest of the score, which was not written by Bach, is a copy of the lost original score X. Thus it is also based on Version I, and in fact far more closely than the autograph section, for the notion that the copyist made improvements and alterations can be excluded. Of course, it is quite conceivable that Bach also made changes to X after 1724, which now appear in A as uncorrected original entries. This is true, for example, of movement 33, which appears in A in the longer version that we know from Versions II and IV. Significantly, Bach had to step in when it came to writing the continuo. It seems that the alterations in X had made it illegible.

Finally, Bach revised the section written by the copyist, though he did not examine it all in the same detail. Some movements were carefully revised, though the majority were either checked superficially or not at all.

This suggests an obvious conclusion. Bach's final revision of the Passion was never completed. Most of its readings never found their way into the original set of parts, and thus were never played during Bach's lifetime. The inconsistent perusal of the section of the score written by the copyist certainly cannot pass for the revision that never took place.

It is difficult to say why Bach broke off work on the new copy. Mendel, *KB* (p. 75) refers to the well-known incident on 17 March 1739. The Council servant brings Bach the news that 'the music he was planning to perform on the forthcoming Good Friday was not to be played until he had received due permission to do so, whereupon the latter replied that it had always been done thus, it was of no particular interest to him, for it did him no good whatsoever, and it was only a burden. He would tell the superintendent that he had been forbidden to perform it. If there were objections to the text, why, it had already been performed several times before.'

Bach normally made a new copy of a score only for a forthcoming performance. However, the 1739 incident is only one of the possible reasons why the work was discontinued. The following questions need to be asked:

> Would the time from 17 to 27 March (Good Friday) have sufficed for the completion of the score and for copying a new set of parts?
> Did Bach, if he in fact discontinued work on the score in 1739, perform no Passion at all? Did he perform a different work? Or did he perform the St John Passion after all, using an older set of parts?

Lack of time could also have led Bach to discontinue work on the copy, though this would not necessarily have been in 1739.

An examination of the watermarks involved points to a date that is very close to this, 18 January 1740 (see Ch. II.2 and Weiß, 105). This would seem to confirm Mendel's hypothesis, though it does not exclude the adjacent years, especially 1740.

Finally, the state of the score creates problems when it comes to producing an edition of the work, and for modern performances.

*Producing an Edition*

The 'cleanest' solution would of course be to publish two separate versions: the one transmitted in the original parts (and in the section of score A not in Bach's hand), and the other transmitted in the autograph section of score A. Some scholars have in fact suggested that this should be done.[14] But even if we disregard the fact that such a publication could not be used for a performance (see below), there are other problems which suggest that a differentiated edition of this kind is not the ideal solution. For example, the autograph section of the score has no transverse flutes, and movement 9 contains no scoring indications.[15] Presumably this was merely an oversight on Bach's part that was occasioned by the state of the original score and which is easy to rectify with reference to the original set of parts. However, a new edition that sets out to make a precise distinction between the various source layers must print Bach's discontinued revision without transverse flutes. This would be tantamount to sanctioning something that is quite improbable merely in order to adhere to certain predetermined principles.[16]

Thus it would be much better if the editor were to reproduce the results of his critical scrutiny of the sources in the form of a publication that can be used for performances, and to include a detailed account of the transmission in a critical report—instead of merely editing the raw material and leaving the task of piecing together a version of the work capable of being used by the would-be performer.

*Modern Performance Practice*

With reference to specific details it is possible to demonstrate that the changes in the autograph section of the score do not constitute a significantly different version, if by this we mean changes in the composer's whole attitude to the work. Rather, they are minor improvements and subtle emendations that should not be discarded unless it is absolutely necessary to do so. As in the case of Mozart's Requiem and many other works of a similar kind, the fragmentary character of the

[14] e.g., Christoph Wolff, in Kurt von Fischer (ed.), *Bach im 20. Jahrhundert: Bericht des Symposiums Kassel, 1984* (Kassel, 1985), 13: 'I am of the opinion that . . . that which is fragmentary should remain fragmentary.'

[15] See App. I.

[16] The strikingly similar state of affairs in Part 2 of the Christmas Oratorio (see App. I) has not as yet led to a call for the separate publication of the version presented in the score (which does not include flutes).

revised version will simply have to be accepted for what it is. Whenever score A fails to give the performer the information he needs, he will in principle rely on Version IV of the original parts, though with the proviso that Bach's initial intentions must take precedence over what were presumably makeshift measures. Certain examples of this are discussed in Chapter III. 5 below.

# II

# Transmission

This chapter is devoted to the description and interpretation of the sources, and is primarily intended for readers interested in source studies.

### 1. THE LOST ORIGINAL SCORE X (1724?)

We do not know when Bach began to work on the St John Passion. However, the first version was probably completed in 1724. On this subject see Chapter III. 3 (p. 56).

It is legitimate to assume that score X, which was no doubt entirely in the composer's hand, corresponded in principle to Version I. This in turn is documented by a number of parts (see below), though it must be borne in mind that these include some minor alterations which Bach may have made when writing out or revising them.

However, certain questions concerning the precise nature of X remain unanswered. In particular, there is uncertainty about the participation of transverse flutes (see App. I). Bach may have decided to include transverse flutes in the course of writing X. However, he may well have done so only when he wrote out the parts; and he certainly decided to include transverse flutes in 1725 when he made the revisions contained in Version II.

A series of alterations and emendations were probably made to X in the course of the revivals of the Passion in Versions II and III. They were probably the reason why, towards the end of the 1730s, Bach embarked on making a new copy of the score (A, see below). The fact that Bach then entrusted the completion of this new copy to a copyist enables us to draw further conclusions about the nature of score X, admittedly in its partly revised state.

Obviously, a reconstruction of score X with its specific readings and idiosyncrasies, however approximate, is impossible. Mendel, *KB*, 62–5, includes a list of peculiarities that can be deduced from the evidence of the surviving sources. In the process it transpires that the copyist did not always find the score easy to decipher. As might have been expected, this demonstrates that it must have been wholly or largely a first draft.

As an example of what can be deduced from the surviving source material, the reader is referred to the remarks on movement 33 in Appendix II. It seems that X originally contained the three-bar version of Version I, which at a later stage, and most probably in 1725, was changed into the seven-bar version transmitted in score A. This was written either on an inserted sheet of paper, or copied in an empty space. It confirms that A, although it is probably a copy of X, does not represent the readings of Version I throughout. Thus the latter can only be reconstructed in a reliable manner on the basis of the original readings of the parts in Set I, which have survived only in fragmentary form.

After score A had been produced, the original manuscript X was no longer indispensable, and thus it is understandable why it has not survived. However, it would be rash to assume that Bach himself destroyed it. We know of several cases in which Bach gave his pupils an older manuscript so that they could make a copy of it—after he himself had procured a new personal copy. The most well-known example is that of the St Matthew Passion. Here Bach's later son-in-law Johann Christoph Altnickol (who was his pupil from 1744 to 1748) made a copy of the early version (see *NBA* II/5a), although Bach himself had possessed a magnificent fair copy of the new version since 1736. However, he was probably not in the habit of lending this to other people. If we now no longer possess a copy of X, this certainly does not prove that such a copy was never made in the past. Numerous sources of this kind are no longer extant.

## 2. THE REVISED SCORE (SOURCE A, C.1739/1749)

The facts pertaining to the origins of this score have been stated above (Ch. I). In 1841, having passed from Carl Philipp Emanuel Bach (1714–88) via his heirs to the collector Georg Poelchau (1773–1838), it came into the possession of the Königliche Bibliothek in Berlin, and is now in the Staatsbibliothek zu Berlin—Preußischer Kulturbesitz (Mus. ms. Bach P 28).

Score A, fo. $6^{r}$, movement 2, bars $11^{b}$–30. The words of Jesus, 'Wen suchet ihr', are emphasized by the use of Roman script. The first word (b. 16: 'Wen') was changed from Gothic script. Note the emendation in b. 27 (Tenore), where the penultimate note (here 'zurücke'; in the parts, 'zurück') is changed from e♮ to d♭', which for the first time renders the idea of going backward (a version that was never sung in Bach's performances!).

The score (without later title pages) originally comprised 46 folios that were arranged as follows:

(a) 1 binio (2 interleaved sheets) = fos. 1–4. 34 × 20.5 cm. WM: ornament over ICH in panel, no countermark (Weiß, 133)
(b) 4 sheets (arranged consecutively) = fos. 5–12. 34.5 × 20.5 cm. WM: crossed pickaxe and hammer over a small ornament in a cartouche on chain-lines, no countermark (Weiß, 105). Used by Bach 18. 1. 1740 (*Dok.* i, no. 28, p. 76)
(c) 4 quaternions (each with 4 interleaved sheets) and 1 sheet = fos. 13–46. 34.5 × 20.5 cm. WM: large heraldic coat of arms of Schönburg in both sheets, double paper (each with 2 watermarks superimposed; Weiß, 72)

Scribe, fos. 1–10: Johann Sebastian Bach; fos. 11–46: copyist from the last years of Bach's life—*Hauptkopist* (principal copyist) H—with emendations by Bach.

It is clear that Bach himself prepared the paper, first to fo. 4, and then to fo. 12. The rest he probably added or had added when work on the manuscript resumed *c.*1749.

An original wrapper does not exist, nor has one survived with the parts. The short title reads:

J. J. Passio secūdū Joañē â 4 Voci. 2 Oboe. 2 Violini, Viola è Cont. | di J. S. Bach.

It fails to mention transverse flutes and the instruments required later in specific movements—violas d'amore, lute, and viola da gamba.

Although, as far as one can tell, it is in principle a copy based on X, the autograph section of A nevertheless contains numerous emendations, e.g. the distinction made at the beginning in the continuo, which originally consisted only of tapping quavers, between quavers and crotchets (marking the strong beats of the bar), to which were added the names of the instruments.

The autograph part of the score terminates in the middle of movement 10, bar 42[a] at the end of fo. 10[v] (see the facsimile in *NBA*).

That the rest of the score was written about (or perhaps exactly) ten years later is demonstrated by a number of features that it has in common with the original parts of Version IV—the typical late handwriting of Bach's additions,[1] the *Hauptkopist* H as scribe, and the Schönburg coat of arms as WM.

On account of the fact that score X is no longer extant, the assumption that the autograph section of A incorporates certain changes and is otherwise, in the section written by the copyist, a faithful copy of X must remain a hypothesis. However, everything speaks in its favour and nothing against it. In particular, there are no copying mistakes of the kind that occur when copying from parts (displacement of bars between different systems), whereas mistakes of the kind that creep in when copying from a score (interchanged systems, omission of bars) do in fact occur.

## 3. THE ORIGINAL PARTS

### *General Introduction*

After Bach's death the performing parts of the St John Passion were inherited by his son, Carl Philipp Emanuel. From his estate they passed into the possession of the Berlin Singakademie, which in turn sold them to the Royal Library in Berlin in 1854/5. They are now in the Staatsbibliothek zu Berlin—Preußischer Kulturbesitz (Mus. ms. Bach St 111). The part entitled 'Basso Petrus & Pilatus' remained at the Singakademie by mistake. It is no longer extant, though the SBB possesses a photocopy of it.

If we disregard certain specific problems, then the extant parts constitute a grouping that was correctly understood as early as 1863 by Wilhelm Rust, the editor of the Passion in the old Bach Complete Edition (BG 12: 1):

1. A single set of parts (without duplicates)
2. Duplicates, namely ripieno parts for the singers and the usual Leipzig number of second parts for violin I and II, and continuo (one of each, continuo untransposed)
3. Later supplementary parts and inserts.

A fourth group is formed not by separate parts, but by a number of inserts in the parts of groups 1 and 2. These are discussed below (in connection with Version III).

[1] In particular in movement 33, bc, from b. 4 onwards, and also in movement 39, bc, bb. 72$^{b}$–78 (*Hauptkopist* H may have left them because they were illegible). However, a number of additions could also have been entered at a later date.

The parts may well have been written in the following order. The single set of parts (group 1) was written out first, whereas the duplicates (group 2) were added for a subsequent performance, and the supplementary parts (group 3) thereafter at a later date. This chronology was in fact generally accepted until 1957. It rested on the similarity referred to above between WM Weiß, 28 (Brandenburg Concertos, Well-Tempered Clavier I) and Weiß, 29 (Eastertide cantatas, St John Passion), which led scholars to assume that Bach had had the parts of group 1 copied out in Cöthen because he was expecting to perform the Passion in Leipzig on Good Friday, 1723, either as the newly appointed cantor of St Thomas's, or as someone helping to bridge the gap before a new cantor was elected (see above, Ch. I).

That this chronology is incorrect, and quite unexpectedly so, is demonstrated by two incontrovertible observations, namely the place of the parts, on the basis of their distinguishable features, in the general chronology of Bach's Leipzig vocal works (see Dürr, *Chr*², *passim*) and the particular state of the parts in groups 1 and 2. It transpires from this that group 2, unlike group 1, went through an additional stage (see Mendel, *KB*, in particular pp. 24–30; and the description of the parts below).

If the parts in group 2 thus turn out to be the oldest surviving source of the Passion, then what, we are led to ask, happened to the other parts, that is, the single set of parts which had to be replaced by a new set at the next performance. Of course, this question can only be answered hypothetically. However, from a series of similar cases[2] it is possible to deduce that around 1724/5 Bach evidently lent out several sets of parts—without the duplicates (which was the usual practice)—and that they were never returned. One of these cases is particularly well documented. On the score of the Sanctus, BWV 232$^{III}$, which later became part of the B minor Mass, Bach noted: 'NB. Die Parteyen sind in Böhmen bey Graff Sporck' (NB. The parts are in Bohemia with Count Sporck). In this case Bach also had to supplement the extant duplicates with a new set of parts for a later performance at Easter 1727 (see Dürr, *Chr*², 77 and 93, and Schulze, *St.* 114). Something of this kind seems to have happened with the parts of the St John Passion; Bach lent them out either to Count Sporck or to someone else. Giving away the old parts may have seemed that much easier because he was in any case planning to make a series of changes for the forthcoming performance of the Passion.

[2] BWV 232$^{III}$, 31, 37, and perhaps 172. For a discussion of the issues involved see Alfred Dürr, 'Neue Erkenntnisse zu Kantate BWV 31', *BJ* (1985), 155–9: at 158–9.

There now follows a general description of the parts. As always, the reader is referred to Mendel, *KB* for further details.

Methodology used in the description of the parts. The starting-point is the original state (inferred if necessary). Subsequent alterations are only described in general terms. The gatherings are designated by Roman numerals (I = single sheet; II = binio, etc.), whereas Arabic numerals are used to designate single leaves. In order to avoid confusion, where there is more than one part for the same instrument, these are indicated by small superscript numbers that signify the group of parts, e.g. violin $I^{I}$, violin $I^{II}$, etc. Anonymous scribes are referred to as in Dürr, *Chr*[2].

*Set I*

Page format: 35.5 × 21.5 cm. WM: IMK in lettering panel. Countermark: small half-moon (Weiß, 97). Exists in original sources dated 1723 (BWV 186) and 1724 (BWV 154). The vocal parts contain the choral movements and tacet marks for the solo movements. The instrumental parts contain all of the music for the instrument in question. The details are as follows:

Soprano ripieno. Gathering: IV. Scribe: Anonymous Ia, text in part by Johann Andreas Kuhnau, Bach's principal copyist in the years 1723–5
Alto ripieno. Gathering: III, Scribe: not known
Tenore ripieno. Gathering: IV. Scribe: Christian Gottlob Meißner; text in part by Kuhnau
Basso ripieno. Gathering: I + II + I. Scribe: Anonymous Ic
Violino I. Gathering: IV. Scribe: Anonymous II
Violino II. Gathering: III. Scribe: Anonymous Io
Continuo, Gathering: III + II. Scribe: Johann Christian Köpping.

The original entries transmit Version I of the Passion (see above, Ch. I).

Subsequent alterations in the form of cuts, erasures, inserted sheets, and references, in part to material that is no longer extant, can be summarized as follows:

Movement 1 in brackets. Brackets later removed. A movement that was to be played in its stead (doubtless movement $1^{II}$), which was obviously notated on inserted sheets, is no longer extant.
After movement 11, in the continuo, later autograph addition of movement $11^{+}$, 'Himmel reiße'. Tacet indications added in the other parts. All of this subsequently deleted.
Movement $12^{c}$ shortened to 9 bars and later restored to its original length.

Movements 13 and 19–20 replaced by movements $13^{II}$, 'Zerschmettert mich', and $19^{II}$, 'Ach windet euch nicht so' and later restored.
Movement 24 transposed down a tone and later restored to original key.
Movement 33 enlarged from 3 to 7 bars, and subsequently deleted with movements 34 and 35, partly replaced with a reference to a 'Sinfonia', though in the end restored in its 7-bar version together with movements 34 and 35.
Movement 40 replaced by movement $40^{II}$, 'Christe, du Lamm Gottes'. This was subsequently deleted and movement 40 restored.

*Set II*

Page format: 34 × 21 cm. Watermark: crossed swords with crown between twigs, between chain-lines, no countermark (Weiß, 29). Not recorded in dated original sources. Inferred use by Bach: 25. 3. 1725 to 22. 4. 1725.

Principal scribe in this set of parts is Johann Andreas Kuhnau. The other scribes mentioned below only made minor contributions. The details are as follows:

Soprano concertante. Gathering: 2 II. Scribes: Kuhnau, Johann Heinrich Bach
Alto concertante. Gathering: II + II. Scribes: Kuhnau, J. H. Bach
Tenore Evangelista. Gathering: 3 III + I. Scribes: Kuhnau, J. H. Bach
Basso Jesus. Gathering: 2 II + I. Scribes: Kuhnau, J. H. Bach
Flauto traverso I. Gathering: 2 II. Scribes: Kuhnau, J. S. Bach, J. H. Bach
Flauto traverso II. Gathering: 2 II. Scribes: Kuhnau, Meißner, J. S. Bach, J. H. Bach
Oboe I. Gathering: 2 II. Scribes: Kuhnau, Anonymous Ip
Oboe II. Gathering: 2 II. Scribes: J. H. Bach, Kuhnau, J. S. Bach, Anonymous Ip
Violino I. Gathering: 2 II. Scribes: Kuhnau, Anonymous Ip
Violino II. Gathering: 2 II. Scribes: Kuhnau, Anonymous Ip
Viola. Gathering: 2 II. Scribes: Kuhnau, Anonymous Ip
Continuo. Gathering: 4 II. Scribes: Kuhnau, Anonymous IIe, Anonymous Ip.

The original entries transmit Version II of the Passion (see above, Ch. I).

The subsequent alterations, which were similar to those in Set I, can be summarized as follows:

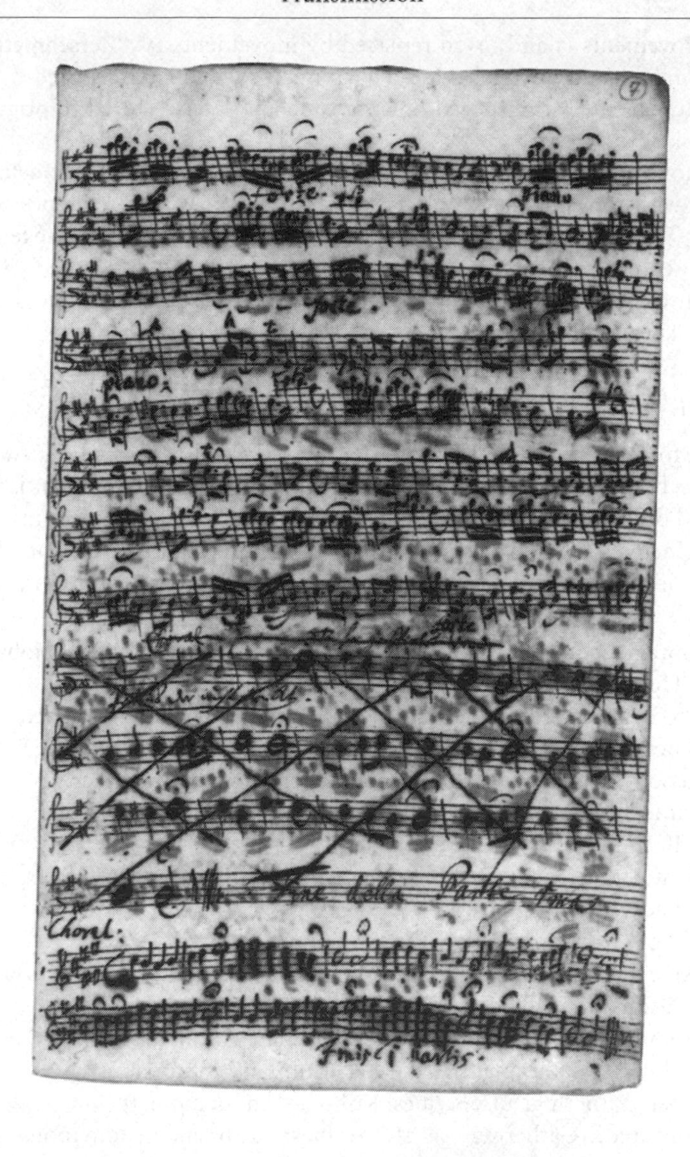


From the Violino I[I] part, movements 13 (b. 44) to 14. First scribe: Anonymous II. For Version III movement 13 placed in square brackets, movement 14 transposed down a tone. For Version IV square brackets erased (but still visible at the end of movement 13). Movement 14 crossed out and repeated in original key below (late autograph in a clumsy and trembling hand).

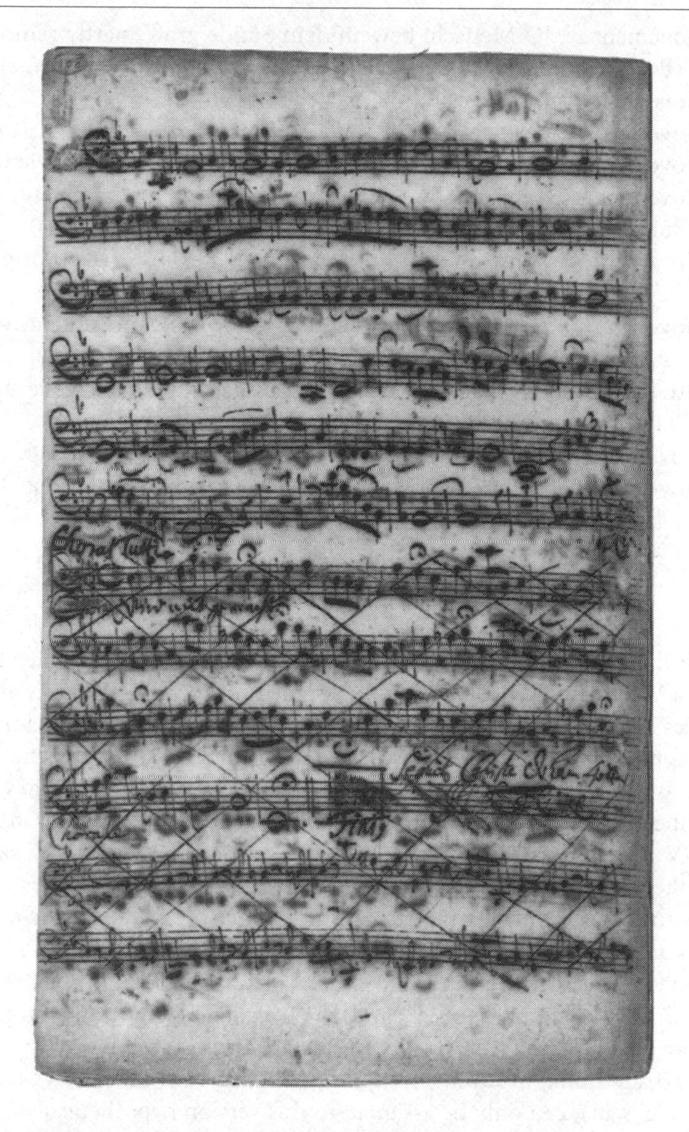

From the Continuo $\mathrm{I}^{\mathrm{I}}$ part, movements 39 (bar 71) to 40 and $40^{\mathrm{II}}$ (to bar 11). First scribe: J. C. Köpping. For Version II movement 40 placed in square brackets and movement $40^{\mathrm{II}}$ added later (Anonymous Ip; rest of movement lost). For Version III movements 40 and $40^{\mathrm{II}}$ crossed out together (the Passion ended with movement 39). For Version IV late autograph comment on movement 40, 'Wird mit gemacht' (Is also to be played), and, at the end of the movement, 'Finis'.

Movement 1$^{II}$, 'O Mensch, bewein dein Sünde groß', partly removed (flutes, oboes, viola), partly deleted and replaced with movement 1.
Movement 9 supplied with text of Version IV.
Movement 11$^{+}$ deleted.
Movement 12$^{c}$ shortened to 9 bars and later restored to its full length.
Movement 13$^{II}$ replaced by a tenor aria that is no longer extant, and subsequently replaced by movement 13 (new inserted sheets).
Movement 14 transposed down a tone and later restored to original key.
Movement 19$^{II}$ replaced by movements 19–20. These movements were later supplied with the text of Version IV.
Movements 33–5 deleted, partly replaced with a reference to a 'Sinfonia', and later restored.
Movement 39 supplied with a different text, probably after 1750.
Movement 40$^{II}$ deleted and replaced with movement 40, probably at a later date.

*Set III*

With the exception of the two parts described below, which, since they lack a WM, can only tentatively be assigned to Version III, the changes in this version were made with the help of inserts. Their page format (except in cases where a page was cut and trimmed) is 34 × 21.5 cm. The WM is MA (or AM), medium-sized letters, each on chain-lines, no countermark (Weiß, 122). Recorded use in dated original sources in 1727 (BWV 198) and 1729 (BWV 226, 174). The principal scribe is J. S. Bach, together with a number of copyists.

With the help of these inserts a number of changes were made in the parts of Sets I and II, in particular the replacement of movements 1$^{II}$ and 19$^{II}$ by 1 and 19–20 in Set II, and probably the interpolation of the lost movements 13$^{III}$ in place of 13$^{II}$, and 33$^{III}$, presumably a sinfonia, in place of movements 33–5 (see Ch. I).

Two additional inserted sheets without WM, each of them 33.5 × 21.5 cm (Weiß, iii), can only be assigned to this version hypothetically:

Viola da gamba for movement 30. One folio. Scribe: J. S. Bach (not in late hand). Evidently a replacement for an earlier part (Version II?). Newly written out presumably so that in the middle section (bb. 20–39) it no longer follows the continuo (as in score A, and no doubt in X), but the alto an octave lower.

Organo for movement 19. One folio. Scribe: J. S. Bach (not in late hand). Evidently a replacement for an earlier lute part (Version I), presumably because no lute player was available. Notated in D♭ major (choir pitch, i.e. E♭ major chamber pitch), a seventh higher than the lute part in score A.—A late autograph superscription, 'Arioso Wird auf der Orgel mit 8 u. 4 Fus Gedackt gespielet' ('Arioso to be played on the organ with 8' and 4' Gedackt') enables us to deduce that the part was either used again for the performance of Version IV, or that it was destined for this purpose (see above, Ch. I).

*Set IV*

Page format 34 × 20.5 cm. WM: large heraldic coat of arms of Schönburg on both sheets, double paper (each with two superimposed marks; Weiß, 72). Does not occur in dated original sources. Used by Bach at various times. The details are as follows:

Violino I. Gathering: IV. Scribe: *Hauptkopist* H (the scribe of score A, fos. 11 ff.)

Viola. Gathering: III. Scribe: Johann Christoph Friedrich Bach (movement 40) and an unidentified scribe

Cembalo, figured. Gathering: IV + 2 II. Scribes: J. S. Bach (movement 40) and J. C. F. Bach

Cembalo, unfigured. Gathering: IV + II + 1. Scribes: Anonymous Vr, *Hauptkopist* H

Cembalo for movement 19. One folio, evidently a replacement for an earlier lute part (Version I), 1 octave higher than the lute part in score A. Scribe: J. S. Bach.

The parts in Set IV include a number of inserts on paper with a page format of 34.5 × 20.5 cm (except in cases where a page was cut and trimmed). WM: IFF. Countermark: stag looking backwards, standing, with spadelike antlers (Weiß, 5). The main purpose of these inserts is to introduce changes into earlier parts. The following have also survived on the same paper:

Oboe da caccia for movement 35. One folio. Scribes: J. S. Bach and unidentified scribe (Anonymous Vc?)

Tenore Servus. One half-folio, with the relevant parts of movements 10 and $12^{c}$ and tacet marks for movements $2^{d}$–9, 11, $12^{a}$, $12^{b}$, 13, and 14 (i.e. also for the choruses and chorales!). Scribe: J. S. Bach.

Basso Petrus & Pilatus. One folio, with the relevant parts for movements 10, $12^{c}$, 16, 18, 21, 23, 25 and tacet marks for the other movements from $2^{d}$ onwards. Scribe: J. S. Bach.

The conclusions to be drawn from the production of Set IV and its inserts were discussed in Chapter 1. It is noteworthy that for the lute part in movement 19 there are two seemingly conflicting substitute parts for organ and for harpsichord, the first probably written out for Version III, though the late autograph superscription indicates that it continued to be valid in Version IV, and the second newly written out for Version IV. A simultaneous use of both parts cannot be ruled out, though for musical reasons this does not seem very plausible. For some time Bach obviously could not make up his mind which of the two instruments he wished to employ.

*Parts no longer extant*

Inasmuch as they can still be ascertained, losses seem to have occurred only in the case of Sets I and III. The following parts are no longer extant, though they must have existed:

Flauto traverso $I^{I}$, $II^{I}$ (?—see below)
Oboe $I^{I}$, $II^{I}$
Violino $I^{I}$, $II^{I}$ (first copies)
Viola$^{I}$
Soprano concertante$^{I}$
Alto concertante$^{I}$
Tenore Evangelista$^{I}$
Basso Jesus$^{I}$
Continuo$^{I}$ (first copy, not transposed, not figured)
Continuo$^{I}$ (pro Organo: transposed, figured)
Inserts in certain movements for
  Viola d'amore $I^{I}$, $II^{I}$ (movements 19, 20, and perhaps 34; see App. I)
  Viola da gamba$^{I}$ (movement 30)
  Liuto$^{I}$ (movement 19)
Inserts for movements $13^{III}$ and $33^{III}$ of Version III. It is no longer possible to say what these were.

In the case of the other solo parts—Ancilla (?), Servus, Petrus, Pilatus—single sheets may well have existed, possibly in order to accommodate the performers concerned.

Whether and to what extent Version I called for the participation of transverse flutes remains a moot point and is discussed in Appendix I.

Perhaps there were only inserted parts for these instruments. If there were no transverse flutes at all, then the question remains of whether there were inserted parts for other instruments, or whether their music (at least in the case of movements 9, $23^{f}$, and 35) was assigned to other parts.

Whereas the parts of Set I probably disappeared because, as we have seen, they were lent out (p. 19) the organ continuo part evidently disappeared at a later stage, after the performance of Version IV. A part written out to replace it does not exist, and the figured harpsichord part of Version IV shows quite clearly that the figures were based on a transposed original. The organ part did not necessarily belong to the single set of parts (which disappeared together with the first copy of the untransposed $\text{continuo}^{I}$ part), and thus when this was lent out it could well have remained in Leipzig.

Only a few scattered references to the parts that are no longer extant have survived. With regard to the organ continuo part see above. Furthermore, the duplicate violin $I^{1}$ part for movement 13 contains numerous ornaments that do not appear in score A, and which thus cannot have been present in X. Bach had evidently revised the first copy of violin $I^{I}$ before the duplicate was copied out, a wholly normal procedure. It may also be taken for granted that Johann Andreas Kuhnau, Bach's principal copyist in the early Leipzig years, bore the brunt of the copying work in the case of Set I (as he did a year later), for his hand also appears in the text underlay of the ripieno vocal parts (see above).

When one takes stock of the sources, it becomes apparent that Bach in fact left the St John Passion behind in a state that was not much more complete than that of the *Art of Fugue*. In both cases there is a first autograph version,[3] and the planned revision remained fragmentary.[4] Bach no doubt originally intended to rewrite score A himself. Similarly, it may be assumed that he was planning to have a new set of parts copied out from score A in order to be able to perform the revised version.

This fragmentary character means that the musical text in modern editions cannot be taken to represent the 'final version' (*Fassung letzter Hand*) in the accepted sense of the phrase, even if we disregard the fact

[3] Respectively the 'Berlin Autograph' (SSB Mus ms. Bach P 200) and X, the version of the score deduced from Set I and from the copyist's part of score A.

[4] On the one hand the posthumous printed version and the supplements to P 200; on the other the autograph part of score A. The extant sources for the *Art of Fugue* make it possible to surmise that Bach planned a thoroughgoing revision of the work; in the case of the St John Passion the extent of the envisaged changes to movements 11 ff. will always remain a mystery.

Insert for the part of Tenore Evangelista, movement 20 (bars $33^{b}$ ff.). In Version III the upper insert replaced movement $19^{II}$, which had originally been entered in Version II. Autograph.—The lower illustration shows the reverse side, with exactly the same bars (notes written by *Hauptkopist* H) with autograph underlay of the altered text of Version IV, and attendant changes to the music.

that it is proffered as a concoction of a number of differing sources.[5] It is of course true that many of the later emendations clearly exhibit an increase in artistic quality. However, in an even greater number of cases it is legitimate to ask whether they correspond to Bach's intentions or whether in fact they had to be made because there was a pressing need to do so. This is particularly true of certain peculiarities in Versions III and IV such as the textual changes in movements 9, 19, 20 (and 39?), the replacement of the violas d'amore by muted violins in movements 19 and 20, and the replacement of the lute by organ or harpsichord in movement 19. Obviously, there are limits when one attempts to apply to the age of Bach the ideal of the *opus perfectum*, or of the *monumentum aere perennius* (the monument more lasting than brass).* A complete autograph score A might also perhaps have found some kind of ad hoc solution for the lack of suitable musicians capable of playing the viola d'amore and the lute. But perhaps Bach would have found a quite different solution, indeed, one that might have surprised us, and which, far from being makeshift in character, would have acquired the status of final validity in the history of the work. That Bach was not in fact unaware of the ideal of perfection is demonstrated by the care he lavished on the production of the score of the St Matthew Passion in 1736. This score affords proof of Bach's ability to polish and perfect a work, an ability that may not have been deployed to the full in the case of the St John Passion. Attempting to come to terms with the fragmentary character of the Passion thus poses a continual challenge to all those who study the work.

[5] Cf. the remarks on this subject in Ch. 1 (p. 12).
* *Translator's note*: Horace, Odes, III. xxx. 1.

# III

# Meaning

## 1. PROTESTANT SETTINGS OF THE PASSION[1]

In liturgical terms, the story of the Crucifixion, the central event on which the Christian idea of salvation is based, forms part of the Gospel readings. These were already emphasized by particularly solemn delivery in early Christian times. Such solemnity was achieved by assigning the reading (which was chanted) to a number of different people (Evangelist, Jesus, and other characters), and by the use of music, either in the shape of a special 'Passion tone', or the polyphonic setting of the turba ('crowd') choruses or of the whole biblical narrative (responsorial or through-composed Passion).

A further element was the addition of sung texts that did not belong to the Passion story proper. These ranged from an exordium or introduction (e.g. 'Hear the Passion') and a *conclusio* (usually a thanksgiving or *Gratiarum actio*) of the kind found in the Passions of Heinrich Schütz (1585–1672), to *intermedii* inserted into the story itself, as in the St John Passion (1643) by Thomas Selle (1599–1663). From here it was but a small step to the replacement of interpolated prose texts, which usually came from the Bible, with versified texts such as hymns, or even 'modern' poetry such as (solo or choral) arias and recitatives. This was the kind of Passion written by Bach: the 'oratorio Passion'.

However, the beginning of the eighteenth century also saw the advent of a new kind of Passion setting. Although it seems that Bach did not cultivate it, the 'Passion oratorio' is nevertheless of importance in this context. The first known work of this kind was the oratorio *Der Blutige und Sterbende Jesus.* Written by Christian Friedrich Hunold (1681–1721), it was performed in Hamburg in 1704 in a setting by Reinhard Keiser

[1] It is impossible in the present context to describe the history of Passion music before the time of Bach. The reader is referred to special studies of the subject, especially the articles on the Passion in *MGG* x (Kassel, 1962) and the *New Grove*, xiv (London, 1980), and to the works listed in the appended bibliographies. English readers are referred to Basil Smallman, *The Background of Passion Music* (London, 1957; rev. edn. 1970).

(1674–1739). A Passion in the style of an oratorio eschews the use of the biblical narrative, and lets the events unfold before the listener in the manner of a religious drama. Its language is no longer that of the 'low style' (*genus humile*) hitherto considered appropriate for sermons and religious poetry. Rather, it employs the 'elevated style' (*genus sublime*) used in opera and oratorio, and no longer merely aims at straightforward contemplation, but at emotional involvement and astonishment.[2] Commented upon by occasional asides in the text, which are stage directions, as it were, individual figures make their appearance and speak: Jesus, the disciples, Pilate, etc., and also the allegorical figure of the 'daughter of Zion'.

The poetic rendering of the Passion by the Hamburg senator Barthold Heinrich Brockes was especially popular. It was first published in 1712 under the title *Der Für die Sünde der Welt Gemarterte und Sterbende Jesus*, and was set to music by a number of important composers.[3] A revised edition of the text appeared the following year (1713); numerous later editions differ only slightly from this version. Elke Axmacher assigns Brockes's text, to which we will have cause to return in connection with Bach's St John Passion, to the category of oratorio passion in the low style, even if 'on account of differences in emphasis . . . in form and content it comes close to the passion oratorio' (E. Axmacher (cited in n. 2, above), 121). The principal reason for this classification is the retention of the Evangelist, even though he presents only a rhyming poetic paraphrase and not the biblical text. However, in view of the fact that the person of the 'Testo' (or Narrator) is certainly not unusual in an oratorio, the Brockes passion, from a musical point of view, is usually assigned to the category of Passion oratorio (e.g. by Walter Blankenburg, 'Passion', in *MGG* x).

The Passion oratorio was slow to gain acceptance, and then only against considerable resistance from the Church, which was particularly opposed to the omission of the biblical text. In Hamburg, the city in which the Passion oratorio originated, performances were initially given in a secular context, and did not form part of church services.[4] There is

[2] These remarks are based on Elke Axmacher, '*Aus Liebe will mein Heyland sterben*'. *Untersuchungen zum Wandel des Passionsverständnisses im frühen 18. Jahrhundert* (Beiträge zur theologischen Bachforschung, 2; Neuhausen and Stuttgart, 1984), 99 ff.

[3] See Henning Frederichs, *Das Verhältnis von Text und Musik in den Brockes-Passionen Keisers, Händels, Telemanns und Matthesons* (Musikwissenschaftliche Schriften, 9; Munich and Salzburg, 1975).

[4] See H. Frederichs (cited in n. 3, above), 7–8, and Hans Hörner, *Georg Philipp Telemanns Passionsmusiken. Ein Beitrag zur Geschichte der Passionsmusik in Hamburg*, Kiel diss. 1930 (Leipzig, 1933), esp. 27 ff.

no reliable evidence for performances of Passion oratorios in Leipzig by Bach. Bach's own Passion performances are discussed in Appendix III.

## 2. THE TEXT OF THE ST JOHN PASSION

### *a. The Depiction of the Passion in the Gospel according to St John*

Biblical criticism in the modern sense of the word was unknown at the time of Bach. In fact, it was customary to listen to the Gospel report in a kind of synoptic manner. That is, when listening to St John's account, it was common practice to think of that of the other three evangelists at the same time, and thus to supply the missing parts of the story.[5] This custom was catered for by the widespread use of an *Evangelienharmonie* (a diatessaron or harmony of the four Gospels).[6] A particularly characteristic example is the familiar compilation known as 'The Seven Words of Jesus on the Cross'. None of the four evangelists gives them all. Nevertheless, the seven words were accorded canonic status in sermons, chorales (e.g. 'Da Jesus an dem Kreuze stund'), and music (Heinrich Schütz). This kind of synoptic thinking formed the precondition for the two interpolations in the text of St John's Gospel on which Bach's Passion is based. They are in line with ancient ecclesiastical practice.

However, this tendency overlaps with a different tradition that already existed before the time of the Reformation: the choral performance of the Passion as related by the four evangelists on four different days of Holy Week, e.g. St Matthew on Palm Sunday, St Mark on Tuesday of Holy Week, St Luke on Wednesday of Holy Week, and St John on Good Friday, or, as suggested by Luther, on Sundays instead of working days. Here there was room only for the unaltered text of one evangelist at a time, and this tradition may be the origin of the plan (we do not know who drew it up) to eliminate the interpolations from Version III of the St John Passion. However, and this is the remarkable thing about Bach's

[5] It is noteworthy e.g. that in the libretto of a St John Passion ascribed to Christian Heinrich Postel (1658–1705) (see below, pp. 44ff.) the words 'Und neiget das Haupt und verschied' ('and he bowed his head, and gave up the ghost') are followed by an aria, 'Bebet, ihr Berge! Zerberstet, ihr Hügel!' ('Quake, ye mountains! Shatter, ye hills!'), in which events that are not mentioned by St John, such as the earthquake, the eclipse of the sun, and the rocks that were rent, are alluded to without reference to a prior appearance of the relevant biblical passage—as if this were quite unexceptional (Bach thought otherwise in Version III).

[6] The *Passionsharmonie* (1526) by Luther's friend Johann Bugenhagen (1485–1558) was esp. popular and reprinted on numerous occasions.

Passion, the free poetry and the choice of chorales show that the author of the text must have thought about the view of the Passion adopted by the fourth evangelist. Clearly, there are traits that we now consider to be peculiar to St John. For this reason a short examination of the theology of the fourth evangelist is called for.[7]

Jesus as depicted by St John is primarily the emissary of his heavenly father, and it is his mission to bring the message of his father to mankind. Like God, the Son was in the beginning (John 1: 1–2) and will be for ever. For this reason St John displays little interest in the details of Jesus's birth. All that he has to say on the subject is 'And the Word was made flesh' (John 1: 14). Similarly, on earth Jesus is always the majestic son of God. He performs miracles and heals (and in St John it is especially difficult to adduce natural explanations for his actions) not because he pities his suffering fellow human beings (for example, he allows two days to elapse when he hears of the mortal illness of Lazarus, John 11: 6), 'but for the glory of God, that the Son of God might be glorified thereby' (John 11: 4). At the centre of his mission is the message which God has entrusted to him, namely the summons to believe in him, the Son of God. This determines whether one is saved or condemned (John 3: 18 and elsewhere). Thus St John sees in Christ's passion not so much the pain and suffering of Jesus, but the homecoming of the Son of God to the Father. Even as he predicts his suffering there is the ambiguous phrase that he must be 'lifted up' (on the cross and through his ascension). For example, this becomes very clear in what he tells Nicodemus: 'And no man hath ascended up to heaven, but he that came down from heaven, even the Son of man which is in heaven. And as Moses lifted up the serpent in the wilderness, even so must the Son of man be lifted up: That whosoever believeth in him should not perish, but have eternal life.' (John 3: 13–15.)

St John's interpretation is reflected in every detail of his account of the Passion. The Crucifixion is an unavoidable transitional stage on the way back to the Father. Thus the prayer in Gethsemane is missing in this context. Jesus experiences no conflicts. Similarly, there is no mention of the kiss of Judas. Rather, Jesus goes towards the men and officers and says to them: 'I am he'. The fact that they recoiled and fell to the ground reveals his majesty even as he is about to be arrested. Jesus requests permission for his disciples to be allowed to leave ('let these go their way', John 18: 8); he knew 'all things that should come upon him', including Peter's imminent denial. The crowing of the cock bears witness to this

[7] See the literature on the theology of St John's account of the Passion, p. 129.

knowledge. Peter's remorse is of no importance to St John, and is never mentioned. Jesus's superiority also becomes apparent in his replies to Caiaphas and Pilate. Many of the questions are not answered directly: he refers to other witnesses ('ask them which heard me, what I have said unto them', John 18: 21), queries what is said ('Sayest thou this thing of thyself . . .?', John 18: 34), or does not answer at all (John 19: 9). A striking feature of the account of how Jesus is interrogated is the way in which Pilate runs back and forth between Jesus and the Jews outside. Thus Pilate appears to be far less majestic than Jesus, who stands in one place, and is only brought forth briefly between the two interrogations (John 19: 5). He bears his cross himself, and thus Simon of Cyrene does not make an appearance (John 19: 17). Even from the cross he arranges for his mother to be cared for (John 19: 26–7). On the other hand, there is no reference to him being mocked on the cross, and there is certainly no mention of his cry 'My God, my God, why hast thou forsaken me?' or the derisive comments of the bystanders, who misinterpret this as an appeal for help to Elias. And again, on the cross Jesus is not the man of sorrows, but the executor of his father's will. For this reason his last words, 'It is finished,' are like an exclamation of joy. When he dies, he does not cry with a loud voice.

Naturally, we cannot expect that the poetic rendering of the biblical narrative in Bach's Passion will correspond to the ideas of St John in each and every case. A systematic portrayal of St John's thinking was hardly to be expected in an age in which, as we have seen, the Gospels tended to be construed simultaneously. For this reason no one will have objected to the fact that Peter's remorse is included (or should one say, 'restored'?) together with an aria which originally bore the title 'Der weinende Petrus' ('Weeping Peter').[8] The same applies to the account of the natural events that occur in the hour of Christ's death. In this case an arioso and an aria, which merely mourn the death of Jesus, add a dimension to the music of the Passion that is not very characteristic of St John.

Nevertheless, the text contains passages which may be construed as a direct reflection of St John's thinking. This is true in particular of the opening chorus[9] (movement 1): the beginning, an allusion to Ps. 8: 1 ('O Lord our Lord, how excellent is thy name in all the earth!'), sees Jesus, in his unity with the Father (John 10: 30), as the creator and lord

[8] It is legitimate to assume that in the St John Passion, where it is sung by a tenor (whereas Peter is a bass!), it is intended to serve as a symbol of a more general Christian standpoint.

[9] See Elke Axmacher (cited in n. 2, above), 163–5.

of the world. His majesty remains unimpaired, 'auch in der größten Niedrigkeit' ('even in the greatest lowliness'). (Also cf. the use of the words 'Herr', 'Herrscher', 'herrlich', 'verherrlicht'.) This is the basic theme of the St John Passion. The Son of God, who existed before all time, descends to the lowliness of the world and returns to the Father. In this context 'lowliness' not only refers to the Passion, but also to the mission of Jesus on earth, which men tend to view with suspicion and reject (cf. John 1: 5, 1: 11, and elsewhere). Elke Axmacher (cited in n. 2, above) (p. 163) interprets the da capo form of the first movement as a symbol of the arch marking this descent and ascent.

It is self-evident that the following movements do not bring out this basic aspect quite so distinctly, and that they refer more to the various situations. The paraphrases after Brockes, which will be discussed below, place certain constraints on an interpretation that is based entirely on St John. None the less, there are a number of allusions to his account.

Movement 3: 'O große Lieb, o Lieb ohn alle Maße'

The movement refers to the solicitude of Jesus for his disciples, for whom he obtains permission to go their way. St John adds the comment, 'That the saying might be fulfilled, which he spake, Of them which thou gavest me have I lost none', John 18: 9, which is a reference to John 17: 12 ('those that thou gavest me I have kept, and none of them is lost'), part of what is known as Jesus's high priest's prayer.

The listener at the time of Bach who knew his Bible would also no doubt have noted a reference to other words of Jesus such as 'This is my commandment, That ye love one another, as I have loved you. Greater love hath no man than this, that a man lay down his life for his friends' (John 15: 12–13). Thus there is a close connection with St John's Gospel.

And finally, the idea of living with the world, which is contrasted with Christ's passion, seems to refer to the words of Jesus, 'My kingdom is not of this world' (John 18: 36), and many similar utterances with which St John emphasizes the difference between being of this world and not being of this world.

Movement 9: 'Ich folge dir gleichfalls mit freudigen Schritten'

The image of following Christ—he is 'the light of the world' (John 8: 12)—and of being drawn to the Father (John 6: 44) is certainly typical of St John's thinking. However, at first sight there does not seem to be any direct connection between this and the fourth evangelist's understanding of the Passion, and in fact there is even less connection with the Synoptic Gospels, for the obvious confession, 'I wish to share the sufferings of Jesus', does not occur at all.[10] Thus the 'joyful' character of the text in a work dedicated to the glorification of the son of God does not seem to be wholly misplaced.

Movement 17: 'Ach großer König, groß zu allen Zeiten'

The first line of the chorale refers back directly to movement 1 (cf. also the fifth line, 'zu aller Zeit'), whereas the word 'Liebestaten' forms a link with movement 3 (see above).

Movement 22: 'Durch dein Gefängnis, Gottes Sohn'

The movement also occurs in Postel's Passion text, which will be discussed below (pp. 44–5), at the same point, that is, after the exchange between Jesus and Pilate on the latter's power to crucify Jesus or to release him, which in fact strengthens Pilate in his resolve to set him free.

That the Passion of Christ is necessary for our salvation is self-evident and not peculiar to St John's Gospel. Nevertheless, the interpolation of the movement in this context introduces a dimension that is reminiscent of St John. Admittedly, this is already present in Postel's text. However, it highlights the contrast between Jesus and Pilate, who wishes to release him.

Movement 26: 'In meines Herzens Grunde'

The beginning of the chorale, if nothing else, corresponds to the opening image of glorification (cf. 'all Zeit und Stunde' with 'zu aller Zeit').

Movement 30: 'Es ist vollbracht'

The text is related to Postel's libretto for the St John Passion (see below, pp. 44–6), and takes as its starting-point the words of Jesus which occur only in St John's Gospel. This and the rest of the aria's text reflect a theology that is characteristic of St John. The words 'O comfort for afflicted souls' ('o Trost vor die gekränkten Seelen') remind us of John 16: 33 ('In the world ye shall have tribulation: but be of good cheer; I have overcome the world'), and the middle section of the aria, 'The hero of Judah triumphs with might' ('Der Held aus Juda siegt mit Macht'), interprets the victorious ending and 'the final hour' ('die letzte Stunde') of Christ's worldly mission as a triumph. This is wholly in the spirit of the fourth evangelist.[11]

[10] In the revised version of the text in Version IV—as might have been expected, one is tempted to say—it does in fact appear in the final line, 'until thou hast taught me to suffer with patience' ('bis daß du mich lehrest, geduldig zu leiden').

[11] Furthermore, in addition to a similar reference to the victorious Christ, the corresponding verse of Postel's Passion contains the words 'in paradise begun already' ('im Paradies schon angefangen'), which also reflect the ideas of St John. See below, p. 45.

Movement 32: 'Mein teurer Heiland, laß dich fragen'

Although they are not as pronounced as in movement 30, the text nevertheless contains some of St John's ideas, e.g. 'livest now forever' ('lebest nun ohn Ende').

Movement 35: 'Zerfließe, mein Herze'

A simple dirge that bewails the death of Jesus, the presence of this aria is justified only by the interpolated passage from St Matthew. For this reason it was excised in Version III. In fact it represents the very opposite of St John's interpretation. Admittedly, if the dirge is in honour of the most high ('dem höchsten zu Ehren'), then he is also glorified thereby. However, it is a figure of speech that Bach's librettist had already come across in Brockes (see below, p. 47).

Movement 40: 'Ach Herr, laß dein lieb Engelein'

The form of address used, 'Herr', and in particular the hymnlike conclusion of the chorale, 'I wish to praise thee eternally' ('ich will dich preisen ewiglich'), refer back in a rather obvious way to the idea of glorification in movement 1, so that the Passion text as a whole traces an arch from majesty to lowliness and back to majesty.

### *b. The Gospel Text*

After this rather general introduction, we will examine the Gospel text used by Bach in the St John Passion.

The work is based on chapters 18 and 19 of St John's Gospel, and in two places includes interpolations that are discussed below. The variants of contemporary Lutheran Bibles that occur are of minor importance[12] and do not need to be discussed here. However, there is one exception. In the case of John 19: 38 the older Lutheran Bibles in Bach's time—and thus Versions I and II of the St John Passion—omit the sentence 'He came therefore, and took the body of Jesus'. Although he may have acquired it only after 1725, Bach owned a copy of the 1682 Bible edited by Abraham Calovius, in which the sentence is given in the commentary. In the Bibles compared by Mendel, *KB* it first occurs in its proper context in 1729 (though this does not exclude the possibility that it occurred earlier in Bibles that were not consulted). It was most probably incorporated into the St John Passion in Version III, and at the latest in Version IV.

[12] e.g. in John 18: 39 the reading of the Lutheran bibles is '. . . daß ich euch einen auf Ostern losgebe' ('. . . that I should release unto you one at the passover'). Bach's setting omits the words 'auf Ostern' ('at the passover').

Mendel, *KB* (pp. 111–12, 150, 159, 281–2) fails to answer the question of whether the correction should be assigned to Version III or IV, and is inclined to come down in favour of Version III merely on account of its 'purified' text. However, the arguments in favour of Version III also include the fact that the *Hauptkopist* H must already have come across the new reading in his model, X. At any rate, he copied it—wrongly, but without Bach's help—into score A. If the reading dates from Version IV, it would be rather difficult to explain why Bach is supposed to have entered it into score X, which was no longer needed for the new version, and on top of everything else so unclearly that *Hauptkopist* H was unable to transfer it to A correctly.

The first of the two interpolated passages occurs in movement 12[c] in connection with John 18: 27. It is a shortened version of Matt. 26: 75. In its unabbreviated form this verse reads as follows (the words omitted by Bach are in italics):

> And Peter remembered the word of Jesus, *which said unto him, Before the cock crow, thou shalt deny me thrice.* And he went out, and wept bitterly.

The second interpolation consists of movement 33, which comes after John 19: 30 (on this subject see App. II). In Version I the interpolation comes from Mark 15: 38:

> And the veil of the temple was rent in twain from the top to the bottom.

In Version II (and IV) this text was replaced by Matt. 27: 51–2, from which only the words 'die da schliefen' ('which slept') at the end of verse 52 were omitted.

The reason for the two interpolations is evidently the desire to make available for the composition of the music affections such as 'remorse' and 'lamentation' (in terms of the contemporary doctrine of the affections), for which, as we have seen, there was little opportunity in St John's account of the Passion. The justification for this, as has already been pointed out on a number of occasions, was the fact that it was considered completely normal to listen to the Gospel texts in a synoptic manner (also cf. the line 'Jesus, also look on me' ('Jesu, blicke mich auch an') in movement 14, which only becomes comprehensible when one knows Luke 22: 61—'And the Lord turned, and looked upon Peter').

The alternative, which is to omit the two interpolations, as in Version III, in favour of the 'pure' text of St John's Gospel, seems, as Version IV demonstrates, to have been no more than a temporary arrangement to which Bach did not accord the status of a final and binding version.

### *c. The Chorale Verses*

Although Bach was not at liberty to do as he pleased when it came to the biblical text, he was in fact able to choose the interpolated chorale verses. Furthermore, he may well have taken the advice of a librettist (on this subject see below, d), though he was certainly not forced to comply with his wishes. The following is a survey of the texts of Versions I, III, and IV, and that of Version II (further details in Mendel, *KB*, 160 ff.). The number of the melody chosen by Bach that is given by Zahn (see list of abbreviations) is appended, as is the number of the chorale in the Evangelisches Gesangbuch (EG) [Protestant Hymnal], if it occurs in this publication.

3. 'O große Lieb, o Lieb ohn alle Maße'

'Herzliebster Jesu, was hast du verbrochen', Johann Heermann (1630); verse 7; Zahn, 983; EG 81: 6.

5. 'Dein Will gescheh, Herr Gott, zugleich'

'Vater unser im Himmelreich', Martin Luther (1539), verse 4; Zahn, 2561; EG 344: 4.

11. 'Wer hat dich so geschlagen'

'O Welt, sieh hier dein Leben', Paul Gerhardt (1647), verses 3 and 4; Zahn 2293b; EG 84: 2 and 3.

14. 'Petrus, der nicht denkt zurück'

'Jesu Leiden, Pein und Tod', Paul Stockmann (1633), verse 10; Zahn, 6288b; not in EG.

15. 'Christus, der uns selig macht'

Verse 1 only. Michael Weiße (1531). Zahn, 6283b. EG 77: 1.

17. 'Ach großer König, groß zu allen Zeiten'

As movement 3, verses 8 and 9. EG 81: 7 and 8.

22. 'Durch dein Gefängnis, Gottes Sohn'

Since Smend (1951: 124–5), this verse has been taken to be the text of an aria by Christian Heinrich Postel (1658–1705). As we shall see below (d), this attribution continues to be hypothetical. However, it has so far proved impossible to demonstrate that it is a verse from a chorale. Zahn, 2383; not in EG.

26. 'In meines Herzens Grunde'

'Valet will ich dir geben', Valerius Herberger (1613), verse 3; Zahn 5404a; EG 523: 3.

28. 'Er nahm alles wohl in acht'

As movement 14, verse 20; not in EG.

32. 'Jesu, der du warest tot'

As movement 14, verse 34; not in EG.

37. 'O hilf, Christe, Gottes Sohn'

As movement 15, verse 8; EG 77: 8.

40. 'Ach Herr, laß dein lieb Engelein'

'Herzlich lieb hab ich dich, o Herr', Martin Schalling (1571), verse 3; Zahn, 8326; EG 397: 3.

The variant movements of Version II contain the following chorales:

$1^{II}$.'O Mensch, bewein dein Sünde groß'

Verse 1 only, Sebald Heyden (1525); Zahn, 8303; EG 76: 1.

$11^{+}$. 'Jesu, deine Passion ist mir lauter Freude'

As movement 14, verse 33; not in EG.

$40^{II}$. 'Christe, du Lamm Gottes'

The 'Agnus Dei' from the *Ordinarium Missae* (German translation, Brunswick, 1528); Zahn, 58; EG 190: 2.

The choice of chorales corresponds to what we are used to in other works by Bach written *c.*1724. Four movements come from the sixteenth century, seven movements (of which two have two verses) from the seventeenth century, and only movement 22, if indeed we wish to include it in this context, from the eighteenth century. Of the movements that only occur in Version II, two come from the sixteenth century and only one from the seventeenth century.

If we exclude movement 22, then the 'most modern' chorale is from 1647; and it is the only one by Paul Gerhardt, whose poetry was slow to gain acceptance by congregations: 'O Haupt voll Blut und Wunden' is missing not only in Gottfried Vopelius's *Gesangbuch* of 1682, but also in the St John Passion.

*d. The Free Poetry*

There has been a great deal of speculation in Bach scholarship about the librettist of the St John Passion. The fact that he borrowed liberally from other poets, together with the incorrect hypothesis that the Passion was written in Cöthen in 1723 (see above, p. 2), has led commentators to assume that Bach himself, 'since there was no poet equal to the task in Cöthen', was the author of the 'madrigalian' sections, 'in which the words of the text, hastily thrown together, had as it were run away with him' (Spitta, ii, 348–9 and 351 [Eng. trans. ii. 520–1] ). Until recently this incorrect evaluation of the quality of the text continued to have an influence on critical opinion. However, it needs to be pointed out that, with a number of insignificant exceptions, it has proved impossible to identify examples of Bach's poetry with any degree of certainty. To be sure, the anonymous provenance of the vast majority of the texts Bach set to music makes all kinds of speculation possible. They may well contain some of Bach's poetry. Yet there is nothing to suggest that the text of the St John Passion can in fact be assigned to Bach, and a remark to the effect that the text of movement 19 'verges on utter nonsense' (Spitta, ii. 352 [Eng. trans. ii. 521]) certainly does not afford proof of Bach's authorship.[13]

Furthermore, it should be remembered that borrowing from the work of other poets or preachers was the rule rather than the exception in Bach's time. This has been demonstrated in the case of Picander's libretto for the St Matthew Passion by Spitta (ii. 175–6, 368 [Eng. trans. ii. 345, 537–8]) and more especially by Elke Axmacher.[14] It was not considered dishonourable to allude to the poetry of well-known models, particularly if one assumes that the author, unlike Picander, had no poetic ambitions of his own (after all, the text does not seem to have been published). Possibly a theologian, he may have considered that

[13] A case that we happen to be able to describe precisely is of interest in this context. In the cantata 'Herz und Mund und Tat und Leben', Salomon Franck's text for 'Aria 3' (BWV 147a/4) is as follows:

| | |
|---|---|
| Bereite dir JESU, noch heute die Bahn! | (Jesus, prepare thy path this day! |
| Beziehe die Höhle | O enter the cave |
| Des Hertzens, der Seele, | Of the heart, of the soul, |
| Und blicke mit Augen der Gnade mich an. | And look on me with eyes of grace.) |

In the only surviving and revised version, BWV 147/5, of 1723, Bach seems to have taken umbrage at the image of Jesus peering out of the cave with gracious eyes, for after writing 'Beziehe die H', he changed the text to 'Mein Heiland, erwähle die gläubende Seele' ('My saviour, take the faithful soul'). With all due respect, it is clear that this kind of alteration is not exactly a good example of what Spitta termed 'utter nonsense'.

[14] 'Ein Quellenfund zum Text der Matthäus-Passion', *BJ* (1978), 181–91.

his main task was to adapt poetry that was both readily available and familiar in order to be able to incorporate it in a meaningful manner into St John's account of the Passion.

The following survey examines the movements which make use of free poetry,[15] and, as far as they are known, lists the models on which they are based. Mere allusions, which occur frequently in contemporary poetry, have been disregarded.

Version I:

1. Chorus 'Herr, unser Herrscher'

The two opening lines are a paraphrase of verses 2 and 10 of Ps. 8. No other models have come to light.

7. Aria 'Von den Stricken meiner Sünden'

Modelled on the introductory chorus of the Brockes Passion:

| | |
|---|---|
| Chor Gläubiger Seelen. | (Chorus of Faithful Souls. |
| ARIA. 1. | ARIA. 1. |
| Mich vom Stricke meiner Sünden | From the bonds of my sins |
| Zu entbinden / | To unbind me / |
| Wird mein GOtt gebunden; | My God is being bound; |
| Von der Laster Eyter-Beulen | From the running sores of vice |
| Mich zu heilen / | To heal me / |
| Läst er sich verwunden. | He allows himself to be wounded.) |

A further verse ('Es muß meiner Sünden Flecken') was not used in the paraphrase.

9. Aria 'Ich folge dir gleichfalls mit freudigen Schritten'

A model for this has not come to light.

13. Aria 'Ach, mein Sinn'

Modelled on the first verse of 'Der weinende Petrus', a poem by Christian Weise (1642–1708). This was included in his introduction to the art of poetry and oratory *Der grünen Jugend Nothwendige Gedancken* (Leipzig, 1675), and is given here as quoted by Spitta.[16]

[15] See the Texts of the St John Passion, pp. 134 ff. On the printed edns. of the Brockes Passion see Frederichs (cited in n. 3, above). The models for movements 19 and 20 of the St John Passion are not included in the 1712 edn. of Brockes. The present comparison is based on the 1715 edn., which, it seems, was widely disseminated (title cited in Frederichs, 16, and in Mendel *KB*, 166 n. 19).

[16] Philipp Spitta, 'Die Arie "Ach, mein Sinn" aus J. S. Bach's Johannes-Passion', *Vierteljahrsschrift für Musikwissenschaft*, 4 (1888), 471–8, repr. in id., *Musikgeschichtliche Aufsätze* (Berlin, 1894), 101–10.

| Der weinende Petrus | (Weeping Peter |
|---|---|
| 1. | 1. |
| Ach mein Sinn, wo denkstu weiter hin? | Ah, my soul, where dost thou think to go? |
| Wo sol ich mich erqvicken? | Where shall I turn for succour? |
| Bleib ich hier? oder wünsch ich mir | Shall I stay? or should I wish |
| Berg und Hügel auf den Rücken? | Hill and mountain to o'erwhelm me? |
| Außen find ich keinen Rath, | Without I find no counsel, |
| Und im Hertzen sind die Schmertzen | And in the heart there are the pains |
| Meiner Missethat, | Of my transgression, |
| Daß der Knecht den Herren gantz verleugnet hat. | That the servant hath denied his master quite.) |

Verses 2–5 did not influence the text of the St John Passion. The poem was designed as an example of how to add a text to an instrumental work, in this case an *intrada* by Sebastian Knüpfer (1632–76), which it has proved impossible to locate.[17] The strophic arrangement of Weise's poem had to comply with the structure of the latter's music.

19. Arioso 'Betrachte, meine Seel'

This was modelled on the first six lines of a movement that Brockes added to his Passion in 1713.[18] Without a new title of its own, it follows the arioso 'Ich seh' an einen Stein gebunden', which is entitled 'SOLILOQVIO':

| Drum / Seele / schau mit än[g]stlichem Vergnügen / | (Thus / soul / see with timorous pleasure / |
|---|---|
| Mit bittrer Lust und mit beklemmten Hertzen / | With bitter joy and heavy heart / |
| Dein Himmelreich in seinen Schmertzen / | Thy heaven in his pains / |
| Wie dir auf Dornen / die ihn stechen / | How on the thorns / that pierce him / |
| Des Himmels Schlüssel-Blumen blühn / | Heaven's primroses flower for thee / |
| Du kanst der Freuden Frucht von seiner Wermuht brechen. | From his sorrow thou canst pluck the fruit of joy.) |

The nine lines that follow were not used in the paraphrase.[19]

[17] Incipit printed by Weise, Spitta (cited in n. 15 above), and Mendel, *KB*, 165.

[18] This demonstrates that the librettist of Bach's Passion must have made use of an edn. of the Brockes Passion that appeared in 1713 or later, and not the 1712 edn.

[19] The line 'Drum sieh ohn Unterlaß auf ihn', which Mendel, *KB*, 166, includes by mistake, does not occur in Brockes.

20. Aria 'Erwäge, wie sein blutgefärbter Rücken'

This is modelled on the poem in Brockes that follows the movement mentioned above. It was also added in 1713:

| Aria. | (Aria. |
|---|---|
| Dem Himmel gleicht sein bunt-gestriemter Rücken / | His back with garish weals is like the heavens / |
| Den Regen-Bögen ohne Zahl | Which rainbows without end |
| Als lauter Gnaden-Zeichen / schmücken; | As many signs of grace / adorn; |
| Die (da die Sünd-Fluht unsrer Schuld verseiget) | Which (as the deluge of our guilt recedeth) |
| Der holden Liebe Sonnen-Strahl | The sunlight's beam of tender love |
| In seines Blutes Wolcken / zeiget. | In rain-clouds of his blood / doth shew.) |

22. Chorale 'Durch dein Gefängnis, Gottes Sohn'

Although Bach set the text to the melody 'Machs mit mir, Gott, nach deiner Güt', it cannot be traced as a chorale verse. However, in unchanged form, so that it is unnecessary to cite it here, it forms an 'Aria' in a St John Passion[20] (HHA 1/2, movement 23) that used to be ascribed to Handel, and which is now thought to be the work of Christian Ritter (*c.*1645–after 1725). Johann Mattheson (1681–1764) set the same passion text in 1723, using the title 'Das Lied des Lammes' ('The Song of the Lamb').[21] In both cases the aria interrupts the biblical text at the same place as in Bach's Passion. Christian Heinrich Postel (1658–1705) is believed to have written the madrigalian pieces of the Passions by Ritter and Mattheson. However, his authorship has been established only in the case of three arias reprinted by Hunold.[22]

The other ten arias, which were not printed, may well have been written by Postel, though there is no direct evidence for this. Hunold's

[20] See Hans Joachim Marx, '". . . eines welt-berühmten Mannes gewisse Passion", Zur Herkunft der Händel zugeschriebenen "Johannes-Passion"', *Musica*, 41 (1987), 311–16. Although there is no documentary evidence for this, the Passion is referred to here under Ritter's name.

[21] New edn. of the score, which disappeared during World War II, by Beekman C. Cannon (A-R Editions, Madison, 1971). For details see Mendel, *KB*, 163–4.

[22] Menantes [Christian Friedrich Hunold, 1681–1721], *Theatralische Galante und Geistliche Gedichte* (Hamburg, 1706), sacred poems, p. 34. Hunold adds, 'The late Herr Licentiate Postel wrote several arias for an earlier passion / and so / because they are difficult to obtain / I cannot resist / including some of them'. He then prints the following arias:

Schauet, mein Jesus ist Rosen zu gleichen
Jesu, wonach dürstet dich
Bebet, ihr Berge, zerfallet, ihr Hügel.
The similarity of the texts was first noted in Smend (1951: 124–5).

phrase 'several arias for an earlier Passion' leaves the matter unresolved.[23] The suitability of the text of 'Durch dein Gefängnis' as underlay for a chorale melody suggests that it may have come from a strophic poem (which had not found its way into a hymnal). See the comments on movement 30 below.

24. Aria 'Eilt, ihr angefochtnen Seelen'

This is modelled on the following aria in Brockes:

| | | | |
|---|---|---|---|
| Aria. Mit dem Chor der gläubigen Seelen. | | (Aria. With the chorus of faithful souls. | |
| Tochter Zion. | Eilt / ihr angefochtne Seelen / | Daughter of Zion | Hasten / ye souls that are tempted |
| | Geht aus Achsaphs Mörder-Hölen / | | Leave Asaph's murderous dens / |
| | Kommt! Chor. Wohin? Tocht.Z. nach Golgatha / | | Come! Chorus. Where to? D.of Z. To Golgotha / |
| | Nehmt des Glaubens Tauben-Flügel / | | Take the dovelike wings of faith / |
| | Fliegt! Chor. Wohin? Tocht.Z. zum Schädel-Hügel / | | Fly! Chorus. Where to? D.of Z. To the hill of the skull / |
| | Eure Wohlfahrt blühet da. | | There where your salvation lies. |
| | Kommt! Chor. Wohin? Tocht.Z. nach Golgatha. | | Come! Chorus. Where to? D.of Z. To Golgotha.) |

30. Aria 'Es ist vollbracht'

A possible model for this can only be deduced in a roundabout way, and once again the information is supplied by Smend (195: 128).

Smend points to the similarity between the strophic structure of this movement and that of the following aria from Ritter's St John Passion (*HHA* 1/2, no. 58), which also occurs in Mattheson:

| | |
|---|---|
| O großes Werk, | (O mighty work, |
| Im Paradies schon angefangen! | In paradise begun already! |
| O Riesenstärk, | O giant strength, |
| Die Christus[24] laßt den Sieg erlangen! | Which causes Christ to be triumphant! |
| Daß nach dern Streit in Siegespracht | That after battle in victorious splendour |
| Er sprechen kann: Es ist vollbracht! | He can utter: It is finished!) |

[23] Here, as in the case of Ritter (see n. 20, above), the movements that cannot be ascribed to Postel with complete certainty are cited under his name for ease of reference.

[24] According to *HHA* 1/2, Mattheson has 'Jesum' in *Critica Musica*, and 'Christum' in *Lied des Lammes* (see Cannon (cited in n. 21, above)).

This text is also entirely in the spirit of St John's Gospel (cf. e.g. line 2 with John 17: 24, 'for thou lovedst me before the foundation of the world').

The connection with Movement 30 is clear. Both texts begin with an exclamation; in the final section both emphasize a triumphant interpretation of the death of Jesus; and both end with a literal quotation from John 19: 30 that has already been heard at the beginning of movement 30. Smend (1951) states that the textual parallels constitute evidence of 'Bach's debt to Postel'. However, as in the case of movement 22 (see above), Postel's authorship, though probable, remains uncertain. Furthermore, on this occasion we are dealing with two different texts that merely happen to have the same metrical structure. Thus it seems logical to suppose that it was a strophic poem, from which Ritter and Mattheson chose one verse, and Bach's librettist another. If the two are reunited, it transpires that the text set by Bach in fact forms the beginning of the poem, for here the quotation from St John occurs not only at the end, but also at the beginning (whose metrical pattern was obviously chosen precisely for this purpose), whereas the text set by Ritter/Mattheson, depending on the number of verses in the poem, was either the second or a later verse.

A noticeable feature of the two verses is the similar turn of the concluding lines, which celebrate Jesus as victor in battle. It leads us to suspect that the poet was reckoning with the fact that both verses would be sung to the same music. But in contrast to 'Durch dein Gefängnis, Gottes Sohn', the strophic structure does not really comply with the requirements of a chorale, and in fact Zahn gives no melody for this text. This would seem to suggest that this is the text for an aria with several verses, and not the text of a chorale. It remains an open question whether it was written by Postel for Ritter's St John Passion (in this case Ritter and Mattheson must have decided not to set the first verse, whereas Bach's librettist must have become acquainted with it somewhere else, though this is impossible to ascertain), or whether poetry by a third person was used by both Postel (and by Ritter and Mattheson) and Bach's librettist (or Bach himself) for their respective Passions.

It is also possible that Bach's librettist wrote an exact paraphrase of a text by Postel, imitating both its form and content, though this theory is not very convincing. There is no plausible reason for such a procedure, and it would mean that 'Es ist vollbracht' fitted into the metrical scheme of line 1 purely by accident!

32. Aria 'Mein teurer Heiland, laß dich fragen'

This is modelled on the following aria in Brockes:

| | Aria. à 2. Mit einer gläubigen Seele. | | (Aria. à 2.With a faithful Soul. |
|---|---|---|---|
| Tochter Zion. | Sind meiner Seelen tieffe Wunden | Daughter of Zion. | Are the deep wounds of my soul |
| | Durch deine Wunden nun verbunden? | | Now bound up by thy wounds? |
| | Kan ich durch deine Quaal und Sterben | | Can I through thy torment and death |
| | Nunmehr das Paradieß ererben? | | Now inherit paradise? |
| | Ist aller Welt Erlösung nah? | | Is all the world's salvation nigh? |
| Gläubige Seele. | Dieß sind der Tochter Zion Fragen:Weil JEsus nun nichts kan vor Schmertzen sagen / | Faithful Soul. | These things Zion's daughter asks: As Jesus naught can say for pain / |
| | So neiget er sein Haupt / und wincket: Ja! | | He bows his head / and gestures: Yes!) |

34. Arioso 'Mein Herz, indem die ganze Weit'

35. Aria 'Zerfließe, mein Herze'

These are modelled on the following movement in Brockes:

| | Accompagnement. | | Accompaniment. |
|---|---|---|---|
| Gläubige Seele. | Bey JEsus Todt und Leiden / leidet | Faithful Soul. | At Jesus's death and passion / there suffers |
| | Des Himmels Kreiß / die gantze Welt: | | The firmament of heaven / the whole world: |
| | Der Mond / der sich in Trauer kleidet / | | The moon / apparelled now in mourning / |
| | Gibt Zeugniß daß sein Schöpffer fällt; | | Bears witness that its maker falls; |
| | Es scheint / ob lesch in JEsus Blut / | | It seems / as if in Jesus's blood is quenched |
| | Das Feur der Sonnen Strahl und Gluht. | | The fire of the sun's rays and heat. |
| | Man spaltet ihm die Brust / die kalten Felsen spalten / | | They cleave his breast / the cold rocks break asunder / |
| | Zum Zeichen / daß auch sie den Schöpffer sehn erkalten. | | A sign / that they too see their maker die. |

| | |
|---|---|
| Was thust denn du mein Hertz? Ersticke / GOtt zu Ehren / | What dost thou then my heart? Choke / to honour God / |
| In einer Sündfluth bittrer Zähren. | In a deluge of bitter tears.) |

39. Chorus 'Ruht wohl, ihr heiligen Gebeine'

Although there are many similar texts for a *conclusio* of this kind, it is only possible to adduce a specific model for the final line of the movement. It occurs in the last aria of the Brockes Passion, which immediately precedes the concluding chorale. In its complete form this reads as follows:

| Aria. | (Aria. |
|---|---|
| Wisch ab der Thränen scharffe Lauge / | Wipe off the briny liquid of thy tears / |
| Steh / seelge Seele / nun in Ruh! | Rest / blessed soul / in peace at last! |
| Sein ausgesperrter Arm / und sein geschlossen Auge | His outstretched arm / and his closed eye |
| Sperrt dir den Himmel auf / und schliest die Hölle zu. | Open heaven for thee / and shut the gates of Hell.) |

In Version II the following texts were added or exchanged for earlier ones.

11$^{+}$. Aria 'Himmel reiße. Welt erbebe'

It has proved impossible to trace a model for this. However, it is noticeable that, with regard to subject matter, rhyme, and often even the syntax, the free poetry complements the incorporated chorale 'Jesu, deine Passion ist mir lauter Freude' (cf. e.g. 'If on the stations of the cross, Thy thorns are strewn and scattered, My soul on roses walks' ('Werden auf den Kreuzeswegen deine Dornen ausgesät, meine Seel auf Rosen geht') ) in a manner that has no counterpart in any other text set by Bach, not even in movement 32 of the Passion.

That this movement probably comes from one of Bach's earlier works is demonstrated by the difference between this version of the chorale and its three other occurrences in the Passion (see above, p. 6), and, as Spitta pointed out (354 [Eng. trans. ii. 524] ), by the text, which mentions the fact that the Son of God has been battered and destroyed ('zerschlagne'), and not that he has been beaten ('geschlagne'). However, at this juncture Jesus has only been struck with the palm of an officer's hand. Furthermore, it refers to Golgotha, thorns, wounds, dying, and 'stormy weather'—all of them events that occur only at a later stage. The text may well come from a Passion cantata. At any rate, the aria only makes sense when it is directly associated with the crucifixion and the death of Christ. It may have been part of the hypothetical Weimar Passion, which has been alluded to above. More cannot be said on this subject.

13$^{II}$. Aria, 'Zerschmettert mich, ihr Felsen und ihr Hügel'
19$^{II}$. Aria, 'Ach windet euch nicht so, geplagte Seelen'

The poetic parallels adduced by scholars hardly ever go beyond the store of words and images that were part of the standard repertory of baroque poetry and sermons.[25] For this reason it is not necessary to print a specific example.

There is no extant documentary evidence for the substitute pieces played in Version III.

In Version IV, the text was rewritten in movements 9, 19, and 20. These variants are given below (pp. 175–6).

There is another example of textual revision in the original set of parts. It occurs in movement 39. These changes were probably made on the occasion of a performance by Carl Philipp Emanuel Bach in Hamburg.[26] However, it cannot be ruled out that Bach's son made use of a text that had previously been envisaged for use in Version IV (though it had not been entered at the time), and for this reason it is also given below (pp. 176–7).

It is impossible in this context to demonstrate that these texts do not fit in with the illustrative figures of Bach's music (see Mendel, *KB*, 169–72); it is merely possible to assess the nature of the alterations. Noteworthy is their low poetic quality (cf. e.g. the repetition of the words 'mein Heiland' in movement 9), the rejection of baroque imagery in favour of rationalism, and the shift from concrete object to abstract concept. Compare Versions I and IV (see p. 50).

It is difficult to believe that Bach would have incorporated these examples of abstract rationalism into the Passion if he had not been forced to do so. However, there is no evidence for any coercion of this kind. As we have seen (p. 41), Bach substituted the word 'erwähle' for the image of 'die Höhle des Herzens', but this is a rather harmless alteration when compared with the radical excision of vivid images in

[25] Salomon Franck's verse 'Ihr Felsen! reißt! ihr Berge fallt!' comes closest to demonstrating a connection with Bach's Weimar period (it is given in Spitta ii. 350 [not in Eng. trans.], and in Mendel, *KB*, 168).

[26] See Hans-Joachim Schulze, 'Die Bach-Überlieferung. Plädoyer für ein notwendiges Buch', *Beiträge zur Musikwissenschaft*, 17 (1975), 45–57: here at 48; and id., 'Zur Aufführungsgeschichte von Bachs Johannes-Passion', *BJ* (1983), 118–19.

the present texts. Nevertheless, it is certainly worth asking whether we occasionally accord too much importance to the rhetorical and figurative dimension of Bach's 'musical language' nowadays. It seems to suggest that Bach's music, apart from serving as a vehicle for the expression of the sung text and its peculiarities, has no artistic value of its own. However, the procedure Bach adopted when composing the turba choruses of the St John Passion should make us wary of defining the essence of his art only in terms of the way he responded to the words of the text.

[Comparison of Versions I and IV]

| Movt | Version I | Version IV |
|---|---|---|
| 9 | mit freudigen Schritten | mein Heiland, mit Freuden |
| | (with steps that are joyful) | (my saviour, with gladness) |
| | zu ziehen, zu schieben, zu bitten | mich lehrest [*sic*], geduldig zu leiden |
| | (to draw me, to push me, to entreat) | (hast taught me . . . to suffer with patience) |
| 19 | stechen | drängen |
| | (pierce) | (hurt) |
| | Himmelsschlüsselblume | Schuld, Isop |
| | (Heaven's primroses) | (guilt, hyssop) |
| 20 | blutgefärbter Rücken | schmerzhaft bitter Leiden |
| | (back that's stained with blood) | (painful bitter suffering) |
| | die Wasserwogen | mit vielen Schrecken |
| | (watery billows) | (with great dismay) |
| | Regenbogen | Lust erwecken |
| | (rainbow) | (give me pleasure) |
| | Gnadenzeichen | Höll und Tod |
| | (symbol of the grace) | (hell and death) |
| 39 | Ruht wohl | Ich weiß |
| | (Sleep well) | (I know) |

To round off the remarks on the libretto, we will glance briefly at the overall poetic design.[27] Its structure is of course determined by the biblical narrative. Theological tradition, both in sermons and in the representation of the Passion, stipulated a division into five *actus*. This order can be expressed in the form of a hexameter:

[27] The following remarks are based on Martin Petzoldt, *Johann Sebastian Bach, Matthäus-Passion* (Schriftenreihe der Internationalen Bachakademie Stuttgart, ii; Kassel, 1990), 50–75, and id., *Johann Sebastian Bach, Johannes-Passion* (Schriftenreihe der Internationalen Bachakademie Stuttgart, v; Kassel, 1993), 44–61.

Hortus, Pontifices, Pilatus Cruxque, Sepulchrum
(Garden, Priests, Pilate and Cross, Sepulchre).

The various sections of this obvious arrangement are weighted differently, partly because it is not specially designed for St John's Gospel.[28] However, it seems that Bach and his librettists included it in their plan inasmuch as each *actus* is brought to an end by a simple chorale movement. The arrangement is as follows:

Exordium I
1. Chorus: 'Herr, unser Herrscher'

A. 'Hortus'
 2. John 18: 1–8
 3. Chorale: 'O große Lieb'
 4. John 18: 9–11
 5. Chorale: 'Dein Will gescheh'

B. 'Pontifices'
 6. John 18: 12–14
 7. Aria: 'Von den Stricken meiner Sünden'
 8. John 18: 15[a]
 9. Aria: 'Ich folge dir gleichfalls'
 10. John 18: 15[b]–23
 11. Chorale: 'Wer hat dich so geschlagen'
 12. John 18: 24–7; Matt. 26: 75
 13. Aria: 'Ach, mein Sinn'
 14. Chorale: 'Petrus, der nicht denkt zurück'

[Sermon]

Exordium II
 15. Chorale: Christus, der uns selig macht

C. 'Pilatus'
 16. John 18: 28–36
 17. Chorale: 'Ach großer König'
 18. John 18: 37–19: 1
 19. Arioso: 'Betrachte, meine Seel'
 20. Aria: 'Erwäge, wie sein blutgefärbter Rücken'
 21. John 19: 2–12[a]
 22. Chorale: 'Durch dein Gefängnis, Gottes Sohn'
 23. John 19: 12[b]–17

[28] e.g. in the *actus* 'Hortus', there is no reference to the Last Supper or to the Garden of Gethsemane.

24. Aria: 'Eilt, ihr angefochtnen Seelen'
25. John 19: 18–22
26. Chorale: 'In meines Herzens Grunde'

D. 'Crux'

27. John 19: 23–27$^{a}$
28. Chorale: 'Er nahm alles wohl in acht'
29. John 19: 27$^{b}$–30$^{a}$
30. Aria: 'Es ist vollbracht'
31. John 19: 30$^{b}$
32. Aria: 'Mein teurer Heiland, laß dich fragen'
33. Mark 15: 38 or Matt. 27: 51–2
34. Arioso: 'Mein Herz, indem die ganze Welt'
35. Aria: 'Zerfließe, mein Herze'
36. John 19: 31–7
37. Chorale: 'O hilf Christe, Gottes Sohn'

E. 'Sepulchrum'

38. John 19: 8–42
39. Chorus: 'Ruht wohl, ihr heiligen Gebeine'
40. Chorale: 'Ach Herr, laß dein lieb Engelein'

The usual *conclusio*, movement 39, and the final chorale of *actus* E, have been interchanged, possibly because Bach decided to alter the original design.[29]

Whether or not this was intentional, the result is a certain symmetry. The framing sections A and E are reduced to a minimum. In the case of E this is obvious, whereas in A it is the result of the fact that St John omits accounts of the Last Supper and the Garden of Gethsemane.

The three central *actus* are not only longer with regard to the biblical narrative,[30] but also have more 'madrigalian' poetry. *Actus* B contains three arias, *actus* C two arias and an arioso, and *actus* D three arias and an arioso. There are no recitatives based on free poetry.[31]

It should be emphasized that the following attempt to describe the probable thoughts and intentions of the compiler of the text is largely a matter of speculation.

The task of a librettist in the age of Bach was to supply the composer

[29] This assumption seems particularly plausible if we presuppose that Bach was involved in the selection of the chorales.

[30] On Bach's composition of the turba choruses see below, pp. 57 ff. (Ch. III. 3. a).

[31] In the St Matthew Passion Bach eschews the term 'Arioso' and uses 'Recitativo' instead, whereas in both Passions the Evangelist's recitative is as a rule simply marked 'Evangelista'.

with texts replete with imagery, each of which had to depict a certain 'affection' (hardly ever more than one) capable of being rendered in musical terms. The story of the Passion as related by St John contains the following possible starting-points: the arrest of Jesus (movement 7), his scourging (movements 19–20), his crucifixion (movement 24), his last words (movement 30), and his death (movement 32). These events are portrayed from a soteriological angle, e.g. the arrest of Jesus from the point of view of the Christian's deliverance from sin ('From the bonds of my transgressions, To unbind me . . .' ('Von den Stricken meiner Sünden mich zu entbinden . . .'))—a peculiarity that distinguishes the Passion from opera. When Bach was appointed to the post in Leipzig, the wish was expressed that he should 'write works . . . which were not theatrical' (*Dok.* ii, no. 129, p. 94). Of course, Bach's compositions are not wholly lacking in drama, as is demonstrated, for example, by the meditation on the arrest of Jesus in the St Matthew Passion ('Sind Blitze, sind Donner in Wolken verschwunden?'). In the St John Passion the poet emphasizes the drama by means of interpolations from St Matthew and St Mark, which provide an opportunity to express the affections of 'remorse' (movement 13), 'suffering' (movement 34), and 'mourning' (movement 35) in musical terms. Yet even here the poet proceeded with a great deal of caution, eschewing a paraphrase of the much more dramatic aria of the remorse of Peter provided by Brockes,[32] and making use of a poem by Christian Weise instead.

Only one aria has an unusual place, namely 'Ich folge dir gleichfalls mit freudigen Schritten' (movement 9). There are several reasons for this. It follows the previous aria (movement 7) after a few words by the Evangelist, refers to a relatively unimportant event, Peter following Jesus, and interprets it as an image of the devout Christian following the example of Christ. The 'joyous' affection of the poetry and of the music signifies a considerable distance from the Passion narrative, which after all depicts Peter's failure and his denial of Christ. The aria would make more sense if, instead of intensifying the image of discipleship ('do not cease, Thyself to draw me . . .' ('höre nicht auf, selbst an mir zu ziehen . . .')), the middle section were to contain a plea not to be led into temptation, or for fortitude in the face of adversity. Finally, a feature of the text is that there is no known model of which it is a

[32] The text is as follows:

| | |
|---|---|
| HEul du Schaum der Menschen-Kinder! | (Wail, thou scum of human kind! |
| Winsle wilder Sünden-Knecht! | Whine, wild menial of sin! |
| Thränen-Wasser ist zu schlecht / | Watery tears are not enough / |
| Weine Blut / verstockter Sünder! | Weep thou blood / obstinate sinner!) |

paraphrase. This otherwise holds true only of the introductory movement, though as a traditional part of the Passion it cannot be omitted. Did Bach himself interpolate the aria into the existing text (or did he ask the poet to interpolate it)? Or did he perhaps make use of an existing composition (which presumably did not come from a Passion)?

Such deliberations lead to the more general question of Bach's possible alterations to the structure of the text. To put it another way, is it possible to unearth a kind of 'original libretto' from under the text of the Passion that we know today?—We may in fact be in a position to clarify at least some of these issues. Thus the paraphrases based on Brockes, if nothing else, can be assigned to one and the same author, and the large number of movements involved (7, 19, 20, 24, 32, 34, 35, 39) doubtlessly points to the fact that he is the 'original librettist' we are looking for. In addition we can surely assign to him movement 1, which, being the Exordium, is indispensable, even if it has proved impossible to demonstrate that it is modelled on a text by Brockes.

We may assign the texts of movements 22 and 30 to the same writer, though not, it is true, with the same degree of certainty. However, it seems likely that he wrote them. They come from a source that cannot be conclusively identified; here it is referred to as Postel. There is some doubt as to whether they were part of the original libretto, a view which is supported by the following observations:

(a) Movement 22 is a 'chorale' in Bach. As an aria it would have led to an unusual accumulation of arias at this juncture.
(b) Its text is not a paraphrase, and was incorporated in unaltered form.
(c) In the case of movement 30 there would also have been a model in Brockes ('O Donner-Wort, o schrecklich Schreyen!'), which was not used.
(d) This movement again seems to be an original text and not a paraphrase, for the metrical structure remains the same as that of the related strophe ('O großes Werk!').
(e) In the case of movement 30 the proximity of the following aria (movement 32) would also have led to an unusual accumulation of arias (as in the case of movements 7 and 9; but cf. (a) above).

It is even less certain who interpolated the aria 'Ach, mein Sinn' (movement 13). Here again there would have been a model in Brockes (see above, n. 32) that was not used; and here again the aria was incorporated virtually unaltered, so that it is impossible to describe it as a paraphrase. And finally, the movement follows on the interpolated passage from St Matthew about Peter's remorse: it remains uncertain whether this addition to the biblical text was envisaged by the librettist, or whether it was inserted by Bach, who would then have selected a suitable aria to go with it.

Of course, it is also possible to object to this argument. After all, the other interpolation in St John's text (movement 33) is the precondition for the following movements, 34 and 35; and that they are modelled on Brockes is undeniable. So at the most we are left with the conjecture that the two interpolations were made independently of one another, the first (movement 12[c], end) at a later date (by Bach?) in order to incorporate movement 13, and the other (movement 33) at once (by the librettist?) in order to justify the subject matter of movements 34–5. In fact it is not even possible to exclude the notion that the librettist at first envisaged the inclusion of movements 34–5 *without* movement 33. In the corresponding aria Postel actually ignores the fact that St John's Gospel does not include an account of the natural phenomena accompanying the death of Christ. At any rate, the fact that the first interpolation originally came from St Mark, whereas the second came from St Matthew from the start, means that it cannot entirely be ruled out that the interpolations may have been made separately.

Thus Bach's librettist was most probably the author of movement 1 and of the Brockes paraphrases, and, although this is slightly less certain, the editor of the 'Postel' movements 22 and 30. It is more difficult to credit him with the interpolation of movements 9 and 13.

The name of this poet remains a mystery. His understanding of the peculiarities of St John's Gospel, which has been referred to above, may possibly suggest a theologian who had no poetic or literary ambitions. It is not wholly inconceivable that we come across him once more in at least one of Bach's cantata texts. On both occasions—and elsewhere in the texts Bach set to music the word occurs only in BWV 124 (movement 4)!—we are confronted with 'Marterhöhle' (see movement 24), a fact already pointed out by Spitta (ii. 349 [not in Eng. trans.]), who noted that the corresponding word in Brockes is not 'Marterhöhle', but 'Mörderhöhle' (see above, p. 45). On 2 January 1724, that is, not long before Lent, when there were no cantatas, and which was thus the time he had to use to compose the St John Passion, Bach first performed the cantata 'Schau, lieber Gott, wie meine Feind', BWV 153. In this work the second recitative (movement 4) ended with the words

| | |
|---|---|
| Die ganze Welt wird mir zur Marterhöhle; | (The whole world doth become a den of torment; |
| Hilf, Helfer, hilf! Errette meine Seele! | Help, saviour, help! Redeem my soul!) |

Of course, such a coincidence with regard to time and choice of words is no more than a fairly flimsy piece of evidence.

It is impossible to state who wrote the new texts that first make an appearance in Versions II to IV. The three arias of Version II are, as we have seen, probably of earlier origin. The aria (movement $13^{III}$) of Version III is no longer extant, and no information of any kind has been forthcoming with regard to the revision of the text in Version IV ($9^{IV}$, $19^{IV}$, $20^{IV}$, and possibly $39^{IV}$?).

### 3. BACH'S MUSIC

By 7 April 1724, the day of the first performance of the St John Passion, Bach had been in Leipzig for a good ten months. Most of the time had been taken up with the fulfilment of day-to-day duties, and in particular with the compostion and performance of church cantatas. Even the *tempus clausum*, the period without cantatas between the second and fourth Sunday in Advent, was in all probability taken up with the preparation of the music for the numerous Christmas, New Year, and Epiphany services. Bach would probably have been able to think of continuous and systematic work on the Passion music only in the *tempus clausum* of Lent, that is, after 20 February 1724, a period that was interrupted only by a cantata performance on 25 March, the Feast of the Annunciation (Lady Day). Of course, the text of the Passion may have been in existence some time prior to this.

Chafe (1982) takes a different view, at least with regard to the St Matthew Passion (see esp. p. 50), though his arguments also need to be applied to the St John Passion. He is of the opinion that Robert Marshall's idea of how Bach normally composed his cantatas—from movement to movement—cannot be applied to the composition of a Passion, for the kind of work based on a predetermined general plan that this necessitated took a great deal longer. On the other hand, it is difficult to imagine when exactly, after taking up his position in Leipzig, Bach is supposed to have had the time Chafe envisages. If we bear in mind that Mattheson, for example, wrote his St John Passion, *Das Lied des Lammes*, in the space of eighteen days (as stated at the end of the score, see

Beekman C. Cannon's edn., p. 173 [cited in n. 21, above], p. 173), then we may certainly assume a similar achievement within the space of six weeks (after preparatory work with his librettist) in the case of Bach, even if we were to concede that Chafe is right to suggest that in the case of the turba choruses, for example, there may have been a degree of prior planning.

The planning, which no doubt began in connection with the production of the text, probably comprised an outline of the whole structure in which the succession of the movements, a meaningful variation in the scoring and the voices, and, presumably, a tonal plan were plotted out in general terms. Some aspects were predetermined from the start. For example, the presence of framing choral movements was largely self-evident. Assigning the Evangelist's narrative to a tenor and the words of Christ to a bass was an old tradition in liturgical performances of the Passion, and, as far as Bach was concerned, not in dispute. The same was true of the choral setting of the words spoken by the 'turba', that is, by the crowd (which included the disciples, the high priests, etc.), so that the distribution of these choruses throughout the Passion as a whole was not something that the composer was at liberty to decide for himself. Furthermore, dividing the work into two parts on either side of the sermon was normal practice in Leipzig, and, being a predetermined division, had to be taken into account by the composer.

With regard to certain other matters, Bach was able to do as he liked. In particular this included the musical similarity of the various turba choruses, which is described below. In other respects, for example, with regard to the formal design, Bach was, as it were, only partly at liberty to do as he pleased. He was of course able to make changes to the libretto placed at his disposal. However, there was a certain tradition with regard to the events upon which the free poetry was supposed to dwell. See above, pp. 52–4.

### *a. The Composition of the Biblical Narrative*

In formal terms the music for the biblical narrative consists of recitatives and choruses. In the St John Passion this division is based on contrast. The Evangelist and individual figures sing the kind of secco recitative that is typical of Bach, and the words of Jesus are not especially emphasized by means of string accompaniment as in the St Matthew Passion.[33] The simplicity of the recitatives is distinct from the turba choruses, the

[33] Bach did not invent this kind of string accompaniment for the St Matthew Passion. It also occurs in the St John Passions by Ritter and Mattheson, and in parts of Handel's Brockes Passion.

considerably more elaborate character of which none the less displays an even greater uniformity.[34]

Bach's recitative, here and elsewhere, is dramatic and expressive. This is seen in the composer's predilection for rich and often daring harmonies, wide intervallic leaps, and sharply contrasting note values. All three idiosyncrasies are more strongly pronounced in Bach than in the music of his predecessors and contemporaries.

Consider the start of the biblical narrative, movement $2^{a}$ (bars 1–8):

Bars 1–8 consist of two contrasting four-bar groups. The first (bars 1–4) contains a description of the situation. It proceeds without modulation in C minor, mainly in quavers, the basic movement of recitative, and, if we disregard a single octave leap, mainly in intervals of a second or a

[34] See esp. Breig (1985).

third, rarely a fourth. In fact the movement begins in a rather high register for a tenor. The highest note of the four-bar group, g', occurs twice on 'Jesus'. The second group (bars 5–8) addresses itself to Christ's adversary, Judas. The harmony has more dissonances, and modulates to F minor. The motion accelerates, and the number of semiquavers doubles, from 24 to 48 per cent. On three occasions the intervals employed now include the sixth, which had been avoided prior to this. But Bach's greatest subtlety is perhaps the similarity between the beginning of both groups: in each case two descending thirds lead to recitation on one note. However, these successive thirds are in sharp contrast to each other:

Bar 1: 'Jesus ging . . .': minor triad over tonic; high register.
Bar 5: 'Judas aber . . .': diminished seventh chord on VII, second inversion; low register.

The increase in tempo (semiquavers) in bars 5–6 and the augmented intervals illustrate Judas's evil activities, which are contrasted with the quiet calm of Jesus.

Bars 13–17, which lead up to the first turba chorus, are also full of contrast. However, they begin with an ascending melodic line, because Jesus (in keeping with St John's image of him) now takes the initiative (bars $13^{b}$–$17^{a}$):

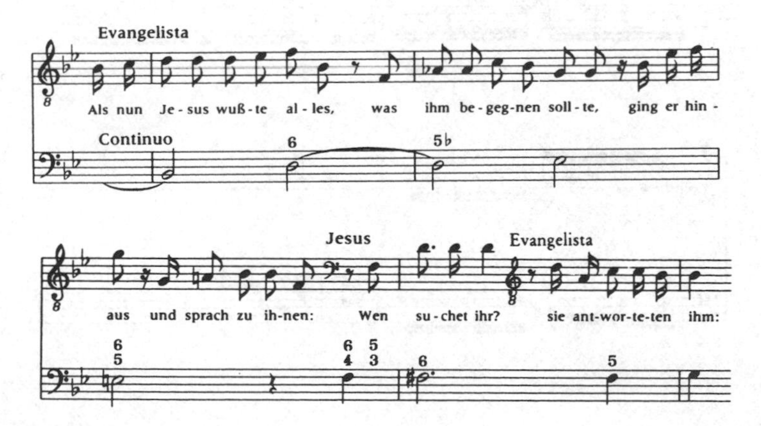


The initial major mode (B♭–E♭) reveals Jesus's inward composure. The sudden chromaticism in the continuo (bars 15–17) with the move from E♭ major to G minor in conjunction with the ascending vocal line to 'ging er hinaus' depicts the change of scene, and Jesus's question 'Wen suchet ihr?' brings with it a sudden decrease in tempo. This in turn reveals that Jesus is superior and prepared for all that is to come.

These insights can be substantiated by comparing Bach's St John Passion with the two St John Passions by Ritter and Mattheson. As these Passions begin with John 19, we are forced to fall back on later passages (the quotations from Ritter are taken from *HHA* 1/2, and those from Mattheson from Cannon, see n. 21, above). John 19: 1.

*Bach*

*Ritter*

*Mattheson*

It is not necessary to comment on the differences between these excerpts.
John 19: 18a.

*Bach*

*Ritter*

*Mattheson*

The account of the Crucifixion, after all that has preceded it, is no longer an unexpected event. For this reason, in all three Passions it sounds more like a narrative than a report charged with emotion. When compared with Bach's setting, the simple manner in which the other two composers treat these words is none the less surprising. In contrast to this, Bach immediately creates a new situation with the unexpected move to B♭ minor: the previous aria had ended in G minor! Even more frightening is the effect of the diminished fifth g♭'–c', the inversion of the tritone, the *diabolus in musica.* And the upbeat 'Alldá' at the start, when compared with the downbeat 'Állda' of the two other settings, also sounds demonstrative and rousing, even though the difference may possibly be due to the dialects spoken in Hamburg and Thuringia.

Finally, we should perhaps take into account the representation of the cross in Bach's setting, which is capable of being perceived visually and aurally:

It is impossible to say what importance Bach attached to such 'music for the eyes'. At any rate, it is certain that he considered the music itself to be of primary importance. However, it may well be that he assigned such notational figures to the category of *adiaphora*, the things one could or could not do as one pleased. Perhaps he also assigned them, as in the case of rhetorical figures, to the category of *ornatus*, the things that embellish speech in a special way and which in this case make it unusually vivid. However, the minimal extent to which this affects the substance of the work can be demonstrated by means of an experiment. If, in the case of the third note, one replaces g♭' with g', the cruciform figure remains, though the musical effect disappears!

We reach rather different conclusions when we compare the utterances of the individual characters in the three Passions. Whereas

Bach, as we have seen, retains the simple recitative style, Ritter and Mattheson often introduce ariosos. It is unclear whether Mattheson was imitating his predecessor (after all, he was acquainted with Ritter's Passion), or whether both severally were perhaps following instructions supplied by the librettist. An example of this is 'Mich dürstet' ('I thirst'), John 19: 28:

*Bach*

*Ritter*

Bach chooses a decidedly simple setting, presumably on account of his contrasting rendering of the turba choruses, which are highlighted by their unusual compositional structure. This is discussed below. The other two composers provide a longer version, and this is followed by an aria, 'Jesu, wornach dürstet dich?', which imparts a soteriological interpretation to Christ's utterance. When we compare the two ariosos, the difference between Ritter's baroque gestures (even if the musical text in bars 4–5 is probably corrupt) and the enlightened simplicity of

*Mattheson*

Mattheson's musical language reveals the generation gap between the two composers. However, a completely satisfactory setting fails to materialize despite the careful treatment the words of Jesus. This is no doubt due to the fact that, compared with Bach, the inventive ability of the two composers was rather slight. Furthermore, the arioso setting of words spoken by individuals points in the direction of the oratorio, whereas Bach's compositional method eschews such drama in favour of a liturgical dimension, and thus preserves more strictly the character of a report.[35]

With the following examination of the turba choruses, which is largely based on the account published in Breig (1985), we come to the most frequently discussed problem in Bach's St John Passion.[36]

The subject of this debate is the compositional relationship of the choral movements and their interrelation by means of a 'web of musical correspondences . . ., in which only two of a total of fourteen turba

[35] There are some pertinent observations on the differences between the work ascribed to Handel and that of Bach in Smend (1951: 124–34).

[36] Breig (1985: 65–6) includes a survey of the most important comments on the subject. In this context Smend (1926) is of central importance.

choruses are not involved' (Breig). This observation is initially of interest with regard to compositional technique, for it provides us with a direct insight into Bach's working methods. In addition there is the question of the consequences for the form of the Passion as a whole, which is dealt with below (Ch. III. 4). At this juncture it should be pointed out that Friedrich Smend's analysis (see n. 36, above), which states that the key to the secret of the Passion's formal design lies in the turba choruses, has hitherto been accepted by the majority of scholars.[37]

Bach links the movements in two ways:

(a) by means of a model instrumental passage that serves a number of choruses as an (in principle) unchanging frame into which to fit the respective choral passages;

(b) by means of parallels between the vocal parts of pairs of choral movements, which are often made possible by similarities in the biblical text, but are not exclusively determined by them.

Clearly, both techniques entail compositional constraints which limit the individuality of each separate movement. Although the parallels between the turba choruses in Bach's St John Passion may seem to be a unique structural feature, the techniques with which it is achieved—interpolated choral passages and parody—are wholly familiar. This will now be demonstrated.

We must first consider the choruses that are based on the model instrumental passage referred to under (a). They are:

- $2^{b}$ Jesum von Nazareth
- $2^{d}$ Jesum von Nazareth
- $16^{d}$ Wir dürfen niemand töten
- $18^{b}$ Nicht diesen, sondern Barrabam
- $23^{f}$ Wir haben keinen König denn den Kaiser

As we shall see, movement $16^{d}$ was later expanded. However, as Breig has convincingly demonstrated, it was originally designed to be just as short as the other movements mentioned above.

The fundamental instrumental model is retained throughout and merely transposed into the required key. It comprises four bars and a final crotchet, and is characterized by an upper voice in semiquaver figuration and a bass voice that indicates the harmony. Both remain practically unchanged, and on their first occurrence (movement $2^{b}$) read as follows (bb. 18–$22^{a}$):

[37] I was prompted to subject the matter to critical scrutiny as a result of the arguments advanced by Werner Breig.

The thematic head-motif, the circle of fifths sequence, and the concluding cadence produce a kind of ritornello passage of the *Fortspinnung* type. The harmonic inner voices are treated with greater freedom, and the instrumentation also changes.

Each of the choruses is composed into this framework, duly taking into account the structure and significance of the text.

There is nothing to suggest that Bach did not design this model for movement 2^b^. Whether or not a plan to reuse the model later on existed at this early stage must remain an open question—perhaps at first it was only a vague idea. In the case of movement 2^d^, which had the same text, it must have seemed obvious to repeat the music. Here at the very latest the decision may have crystallized to retain the model for further use. It seems that the preconditions for its suitability were primarily the sufficient brevity of the words that had to be set; the agitated affection depicted by the semiquaver figuration (for this reason a text such as 'Bist du nicht seiner Jünger einer?' probably did not come into question for such a setting); and, finally, the appropriate nature of short movements in the context. For this reason the cries of 'kreuzige' did not come into question. Restricted to four bars, they would have sounded rather insubstantial.

The composition of pairs of choral movements with identical vocal and thematic material led to the following relationships:

| | | | |
|---|---|---|---|
| $16^b$ | Wäre dieser nicht ein Übeltäter | $16^d$ | Wir dürfen niemand töten |
| $21^b$ | Sei gegrüßet, lieber Jüdenkönig | $25^b$ | Schreibe nicht: der Jüden König |

| | | | |
|---|---|---|---|
| $21^{d}$ | Kreuzige, kreuzige! | $23^{d}$ | Weg, weg mit dem, kreuzige ihn! |
| $21^{f}$ | Wir haben ein Gesetz | $23^{b}$ | Lässest du diesen los |

The similarity of the texts and thus their suitability for musical treatment in groups of two varies. In the case of the two 'Kreuzige' choruses $21^{d}$ and $23^{d}$ the procedure seemed particularly apposite. In the case of movements $21^{b}$ and $25^{b}$ the words 'Jüdenkönig' and 'der Jüden König' provide the cue for the same procedure, whereas movements $21^{f}$ and $23^{b}$ are at the most related with regard to the formal structure, which it is possible to divide in musical terms into antecedent, *Fortspinnung* a, and *Fortspinnung* b. There are hardly any similarities in texts of $16^{b}$ and $16^{b}$ which, as we have seen, were originally not intended to be treated as a pair.

The compositional process in the movements in which the vocal parts are arranged in pairs will seem different depending on whether we are prepared to assume a detailed planning stage before Bach began to compose the work (as Chafe does), or whether we are more inclined to believe that he set the text with due care as he went along. In the case of the former Bach might already have perceived the possibilities available to him when reading the text. As a first step we might be justified in assuming that he made a note of the themes (if nothing else) on a sheet of paper. In the case of the latter, Bach might have become aware of the possibility of composing paired movements at the latest when he reached the first 'Jüdenkönig' ($21^{b}$) or 'Kreuzige' movement ($21^{d}$), no doubt stimulated by the use of the four-bar model in the preceding movements $2^{b}$, $2^{d}$, $16^{d}$, and $18^{b}$. As an afterthought he might then have made movement $16^{d}$, which had initially been composed on the basis of the four-bar model, correspond to movement $16^{b}$.

A third possibility, which lies somewhere between the two already mentioned, is that Bach, immediately after designing the four-bar version of movement $16^{d}$, decided to bring it into line with $16^{b}$, thus creating a pair of movements with identical thematic material. For this reason we will examine the chorus 'Wir dürfen niemand töten' in somewhat greater detail. This is the only movement in the whole Passion which belongs at one and the same time to the categories (a) and (b) mentioned above: it contains the semiquaver figuration and the harmonic model of the four-bar instrumental passage, and also the vocal thematic correspondence to movement $16^{b}$ ('Wäre dieser nicht ein Übeltäter'). In fact bars 42 and $56–59^{a}$ present the four-bar model virtually complete, whereas bars 43–55 were taken from the vocal part of

16ᵇ (bb. 11–23), transposed, and, inasmuch as this was necessary, recast. In the process the semiquaver figuration continued over the inserted vocal passage, and the vocal melodic writing was retained wherever possible within the instrumental model, at least in part (cf. b. 56, alto; b. 57, tenor).

Werner Breig has demonstrated in detail that in his first draft Bach envisaged a setting of the short text within the framework of the instrumental four-bar model, which might have sounded as follows:

It is even possible to imagine an initial version in which the first half-bar of the model does not appear in truncated form (as in Bach's final version). In this case Bach, as early as Version I of the Passion, no doubt cut the movement into two pieces after the first bar in order to insert the parodic passage based on 16^b^. As a result he had to accept the fact that the instrumental semiquaver figuration in bars 43–55, which took into account the vocal lines, was occasionally rather bizarre, and also that it was no longer possible to introduce a complete thematic quotation in the vocal parts of the closing bars on account of the nature of the instrumental model.

If we assume that Bach decided to recast this movement immediately after making the first sketch, and not at a later date, then this, as has been suggested above, could also be regarded as the origin of the paired arrangement of the other movements. At the same time Breig's conjecture that movement 16^d^ was recast in order to lend 'the appropriate musical substance to the weighty meaning of the word "töten" ['put . . . to death']' seems convincing.

Breig has also shown that in all the pairs of movements that are linked by vocal themes, the later movement is a parody of the earlier one. Thus, even if there is good reason to believe in some kind of prescient planning on the part of Bach, seen in this light the work of compositional elaboration was always carried out in the order in which the movements of the Passion were arranged.

If the parodic text was not written especially for this purpose, but instead was a preordained biblical text, it was seldom possible to adapt it to the music without making concessions to prosodic precision, especially in the case of a theme that was to be used in imitation. This is suggested, for example, by the repetition, 'Schreibe nicht, schreibe nicht . . .', in movement 25^b^. Yet on the other hand one admires the skill with which Bach overcomes this problem. This can be demonstrated by comparing the themes in movements 21^f^ and 23^b^:

Whether in fact the theme deliberately refers to Luther's chorale 'Dies sind die heiligen zehn Gebot', as is sometimes claimed, remains a moot point. At any rate, the diction cannot be faulted. Drawing out 'Wir' on a crotchet and especially the demonstrative emphasis on 'dem' seem justified. The Jews argue as follows: even if you, Pilate, can find no fault in Jesus, we have a law, and according to this, the law ('dem Gesetz') of the Jews, he must die.

When recasting the piece for 'Lässest du diesen los', the emphasis on the second syllable of the text had to be discarded, and for this reason the initial crotchet was divided into two quavers. A version such as this:

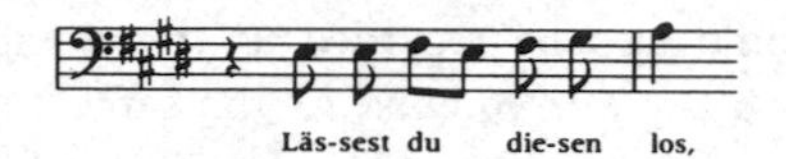


would in fact have solved the problem. Yet Bach went one step further, embellishing the demonstrative 'diesen' with a semiquaver motion. In this way he points to the person of Christ. On the other hand, the syncopated emphasis on 'du' in the following bar reveals the parody character of the movement. It is acceptable, but not absolutely necessary, and accords greater importance to the similarity of the choruses than to the exact precision of the diction.

Only two movements are not part of the web of relationships described above: the choruses 'Bist du nicht seiner Jünger einer?' ($12^b$) and 'Lasset uns den nicht zerteilen' ($27^b$). With regard to their subject matter, they have in common the fact that they and only they do not refer directly to the fate of Jesus, being located rather more on the periphery of the action. In musical terms Bach turned them into pieces that paid especial attention to the text (concessions due to the use of parody were unnecessary), and which in each case and for different reasons produce a decidedly realistic effect.

In 'Bist du nicht seiner Jünger einer?' the imitative thematic entry suggests that more and more bystanders are coming up to ask the question. The ascending melodic line of the theme corresponds to the intonation of the question; and the additional interjections 'bist du nicht' create the impression of insistence.

More vivid still is the movement 'Lassest uns den nicht zerteilen'. A striking feature of the theme itself (movement $27^b$, bb. 10–15)

is that it has a number of segments (four that are one bar in length, and a fifth that is two bars in length). The rending of the coat (b. 2, syncopation), although it is not supposed to happen, then the casting of lots (b. 4, the lots being shaken), and the final decision (bb. 5–6, cadential patterns) are rendered precisely in musical terms. On the basis of this Bach wrote a kind of permutation fugue (i.e. a fugue whose unvarying countersubjects are continually being interchanged), though here it is not the subject and the countersubjects that are exchanged, but the first four thematic segments (the fifth segment, which is surplus in fourpart counterpoint, is a suffix and therefore treated more freely). It creates the impression of a continual stretto.[38] The exposition alternates between tonic and dominant from bar to bar; and as it continues modulations are introduced by repeating one or other of the harmonic blocks.[39]

### *b. The Chorale Movements*

The present account is initially based on the familiar printed version (score A + parts, Version IV). The other versions are examined later. The reader is referred to the description of the chorale texts above (Ch. III. 2. c), which also provides information about the chorale melodies.

The final version of the Passion has only simple four-part chorales. Movements 3, 5, 11, 14, 15, 17, 22, 26, 28, 37, and 40 are self-contained pieces. The only other chorale, which is heard within the aria 'Mein teurer Heiland, laß dich fragen' (movement 32), is also cast in a simple four-part style and added to the aria on a line-by-line basis. Thus there is no need to deal with it separately.

Of course, even if it is possible to call them simple, the chorales are

[38] This density also rules out the impression of a crowd gradually coming togther, as in the case of the chorus 'Bist du nicht seiner Jünger einer'.

[39] See the detailed analysis in Werner Neumann, *J. S. Bachs Chorfuge* (Leipzig, 1950 and later [unaltered] edns.), 44–7.

none the less, within the given stylistic constraints, enlivened in polyphonic terms and by means of passing notes, suspensions, etc. This becomes especially apparent when one compares them with the less ornate movements of Version I (printed in *NBA*, appendix 1). Furthermore, the melodic lines of the accompanying voices and the subtle harmonization make for a particularly compelling interpretation of the text. As one example among many, consider the ending of the first chorale (movement 3, bb. 8–11):

The contrast is spelt out quite clearly in musical terms:

'Lust und Freuden': movement in the accompanying voices (the only passage with semiquavers!), major harmony, with a cadence in the relative major, B♭, instead of the D minor or G minor that might have been expected.

'du mußt leiden': rhythmic retardation, the word 'du' emphasized by means of a diminished seventh chord, a leap of a diminished fourth in the bass, and minor harmony; the word 'leiden' emphasized by means of the dominant of the dominant (instead of the expected subdominant sixth chord) and a leap of a diminished fifth in the bass (or a leap of an augmented fourth in the continuo).[40]

Similar observations could be made with regard to the other chorale movements of the Passion.

In Version I the number of chorales was already the same as in Version IV. However, they were not so elaborate.

In Version II the chorale plays a considerably more significant role. The question of whether this can be traced back to the fact that Good

[40] It is noteworthy that the same chorale has a chromatically descending bass line to the words 'unto this martyr's path' ('auf diese Marterstraße'), which does not require an explanation. Shortly afterwards a chromatic line in the opposite direction is heard to the words '[I] lived with [the world]' ('[ich] lebte mit [der Welt]'). This may well be a reference to the contrast between the sufferings of Christ and living with the world, a life which is quite different to that of Christ, only superficially joyful, and in reality rather evil.

Friday marked the end of the chorale cantata cycle has already been mooted above. It remains unresolved.

The most substantial chorale that the Passion ever possessed was the introductory movement of Version II, 'O Mensch, bewein dein Sünde groß' (movement $1^{II}$), a composition that may well go back to Bach's time in Weimar (see pp. 5–6). Even if one takes into account the length of the twelve-line chorale itself, the size of the movement is none the less unusual. A sixteen-bar ritornello introduces the instrumental themes, which are retained in what follows, though on occasion remodelled rather freely. They are based on semiquaver duplets, which first make an appearance in the flutes and are subsequently almost always present in one of the voices. They were no doubt conceived of as an image of the lamentation over the dead Christ inasmuch as—whether they go up or down, or ascend and descend in dissonant intervals over a pedal point in the bass—they always consist of sigh figures.

In formal terms the ritornello is in two parts:

| | a | a' |
|---|---|---|
| bars | 1–8 | 9–18 |
| | I–V | V–I |

However, no easily memorable theme develops over and above the play of the motifs. Furthermore, the allusion to the melody of the chorale does not go beyond the stepwise ascent (and its inversion) of the semiquaver figures by intervals of a second—surely an intentional image of human consternation.

The treatment of the vocal passages which are inserted line by line into the instrumental texture is not dissimilar to this design. The soprano sings the chorale melody in steady crotchets that are occasionally enlivened with embellishments, and the alto, tenor, and bass accompany it in quavers in a freely polyphonic or loosely homophonic manner. These accompanying figures over ascending and descending scalar melodic patterns (which are sometimes construed as contrary motion) do not coalesce to become independent thematic material or to imitate lines of the chorale. However, they paint impressive images that serve to interpret the text, such as the chains of sixths on 'bewein', the seventh- and ninth-chord figuration on 'all Krankheit', the lunging gesture of the bass on 'schwere Bürd', or the octave leaps in the same voice to 'wohl an dem Kreuze lange', and, finally, the unmistakable cruciform figure on 'lange', again in the bass (bb. 94–6):

This substantial introductory movement has a counterpart in 'Christe, du Lamm Gottes' (movement 40[II]), which forms the conclusion of Version II. Even if it is nowhere near as long as the movement discussed above, it is unusually lengthy for a concluding chorale, for the German version of the 'Agnus Dei' is the equivalent of a chorale with three verses. For this reason it is like a vocal chorale partita. Each of the three verses is embedded line by line in an instrumental texture with its own motivic material. In the middle verse the chorale melody is presented as a canon between soprano, oboes, and violin I.

Finally, the aria 'Himmel reiße, Welt erbebe', which will be discussed below, contains a verse from the chorale, 'Jesu Leiden, Pein und Tod' that is sung line by line by the soprano. With its four verses, it is thus the chorale heard most often in this version. We will have occasion to return to this when discussing the overall formal design (Ch. III. 4).

With regard to the chorales, Version III reverted to Version I, with the exception of the final chorale (movement 40), which, as far as we know, was omitted. Movement 14 was transposed down from A major to G major because the preceding aria was replaced by movement 13[III] (which is no longer extant), but this did not affect the musical substance of the chorale.

### *c. The Choruses*

The St John Passion contains two choruses based on free poetry (movements 1 and 39), both of which occur only in Versions I, III, and IV. Certain aspects of the first of these were later changed and modified. The starting-point of this process (judging by the sources at our disposal) is reproduced in *NBA*, appendix 1, and the final result is given in the main text. The details are not of importance at this juncture. With regard to the question of whether the movement was originally conceived without transverse flutes, see Appendix I. Movement 39 was not noticeably modified.

1. Herr, unser Herrscher

The movement is unusually agitated. A circling semiquaver figure—mainly in the violins, not infrequently in the viola, and occasionally in the continuo—is almost always in evidence over a persistent pedal point. Where it is taken up by the vocal parts, it is heard to the words 'Herrscher', 'herrlich', 'Landen', and 'verherrlicht'. Bach may possibly have construed it as a kind of glorification of God in his abasement (and this is perhaps the reason why it is in G minor). It may in fact be legitimate to go one step further and to construe the dissonant held notes in the woodwinds—here again it is easy to discern cruciform shapes of the kind described above (p. 62)—as a symbol of the Crucifixion, or of the Passion. If this is so, then Bach was obviously concerned to emphasize the connection between the cross and glory in musical terms.

The movement was composed with supreme confidence, and its structure was obviously the result of careful planning. The da capo pattern merely forms the framework for an unbelievable wealth of intricate relationships. If Bach's music is capable of teaching us the philosophical virtue of amazement, then it is in movements such as this.

The introductory sinfonia begins with a cadential pattern, the effect of which is veiled by the introduction of suspensions. It leads in bar $9^b$ (fltr, ob II)/$10^b$ (fltr, ob I) to a canon at the fourth that is based on a chromatically descending motif over a circle of fifths sequence (bb. 11–16: D–G–C–F–B♭–E). The final cadence (bb. 16–19) is enhanced chromatically.

In the vocal sections of the movement parts of this ritornello often serve as a model for the choral inserts, though in modified form. This helps to create the kind of interchange between vocal and instrumental predominance that is characteristic of Bach's mature choruses.

Bach also develops a series of discrete thematic shapes in the vocal part that are interrelated in a number of ways. Its primal cell is the beginning of section A (bb. 19–$23^a$):

α. 'Herr': 3 block chords as a choral insert in bars 1–2 (also: $3^b$–$5^a$)
β. 'unser Herrscher': semiquaver figuration (as in strings)

The block chords are then heard in modified form; they are shifted to the weak beats, 2 and 4, and thus the invocation of the Lord, which is now felt to be a syncopation, becomes even more compelling (bb. $23^b$–24, 40–$41^a$). In addition to this they form the point of departure for a new theme, γ, which first appears in section b (bb. 33–4):

We will come across it once again in the movement in section B.

Finally, section A has a concluding section c, a choral insert in bars 8–18 of the sinfonia, in which the circle of fifths sequence mentioned above is fleshed out with a circular canon (see Werner Neumann, cited in n. 39, above) (bb. 49 ff.):

This also reappears in section B.

In formal terms section B (bars 58–95) consists of two *Stollen* (d d'). Each of the two sections begins with theme $\gamma$, first to the text

'Zeig uns durch deine Passion',

and immediately afterwards to

'daß du, der wahre Gottessohn'.

This is followed in both instances by a three-bar or three-and-a-half-bar insert $\epsilon$ (bb. 66$^b$–69) that is clearly shaped by the text.
It begins as a canon (at the interval of a crotchet) and then continues

rather more freely. *Stollen* d ends with a free reworking of bars 21 ff., whereas d' presents a free repeat of the circular canon $\delta$ to the words 'verherrlicht worden bist'.

The overall formal design of the movement could thus be depicted in simplified form as follows (see p. 77).

The numerous related passages are difficult to represent in schematic

Movement 1, 'Herr, unser Herrscher': Structure

| Bars | Sections | | Formal Technique |
|---|---|---|---|
| 1–18 | | | Sinfonia |
| 19–57 | A | | Principal section a b a' c |
| 19–30 | | a | 2 *Stollen* and coda: |
| | | | 1. $\alpha$ $\beta$ (bb. 19–23ª) |
| | | | 2. $\alpha'$ $\beta'$ (bb. 23ᵇ–27ª) |
| | | | Coda: choral insert in bb. 6ᵇ–9 (bb. 27ᵇ–30) |
| 31–2 | | | Ritornello based on bb. 1–2 |
| 33–9 | | b | Imitative texture: |
| | | | Canon $\gamma$ (bb. 33–6) |
| | | | Outer-voice canon based on $\beta$ (bb. 37–9) |
| 40–6 | | a' | Section a, abbreviated: |
| | | | $\alpha''$ $\beta$ (bb. 40–44ª) |
| | | | Coda: choral insert in bb. 5ᵇ–7 (bb. 44ᵇ–46) |
| 47–57 | | c | Canonic texture with coda: choral insert in bb. 8–18 |
| | | | imitative introduction (bb. 47–9) |
| | | | circular canon $\delta$ (bb. 49–55) |
| | | | Coda (bb. 56–7) |
| 58–95 | B | | Middle section d d' |
| 58–78ª | | d | Canonic texture $\gamma'$ (bb. 58–66ª) |
| | | | Imitative texture $\epsilon$ (bb. 66ᵇ–69) |
| | | | Coda, similar to bb. 21–2, 25–30 (bb. 70–78ª) |
| 78ᵇ–95 | | d' | Canonic texture $\gamma''$ (bb. 78ᵇ–82) |
| | | | Imitative texture $\epsilon'$ (bb. 83–5) |
| | | | Circular canon $\delta'$: choral insert in bb. 10ᵇ–17 and 18 (bb. 86–95) |
| 1–18 | | | Sinfonia da capo |
| 19–57 | A | | Principal section da capo |

terms (for example, the occurrence of the circular canon in sections c and d' or the reference to $\beta$ in bars 70–78ª). The wealth of relationships within the movement is unusual even for a work by Bach. On the one hand, there are the various ways of setting a single text such as 'Herr, unser Herrscher' (cf. in particular bb. 19–23, 33–9, 47–9), and on the other hand the application of three different texts to a single theme ($\gamma$)—'Herr, unser Herrscher' (bb. 33–6), 'Zeig uns durch deine Passion' (bb. 58–62, 78–80) and 'daß du, der wahre Gottessohn' (bb. 62–6, 80–2)—or the application of two texts to the circular canon ($\delta$)—'dessen Ruhm . . .' (bb. 49–55) and 'verherrlicht worden bist' (bb. 86–95). This wealth of relationships already prefigures the web of correspondences in the turba choruses, which thus, even though we should be wary of making such statements, seems slightly less unique in the context of Bach's output.

The structure of the final chorus (movement 39, before the final chorale) is much simpler. Its principal section A, which is framed by a twelve-bar instrumental ritornello, consists of two *Stollen*, a a', of which a ends with a cadence in the dominant (b. 32), and a' with one in the tonic (b. 48). Section a begins with a choral insert in ritornello bars 1–4, whereas a' concludes with a choral insert in ritornello bars 5–12 (bar 8 being freely enlarged to two bars). A second section, B (bb. 61–72, 'Das Grab . . . schließt die Hölle zu', VII–VI), is followed by a repeat of the whole of section A, and is then itself repeated freely and in the dominant. Thereafter a further repeat of A (framed by the ritornello) ends the movement, the (rondo) form of which is thus as follows:

A B A B' A

Finally, the reader's attention is drawn to the peculiarities of the second B section (B'), in which Bach omits the bass, restricts the continuo to two short interjections and assigns the real bass line to the upper strings (violin I and II, viola). Friedrich Smend, writing in a different context (and without referring to the passage under discussion), pointed out that when Bach omits the real bass line and uses what was known as the bassett (the baroque term for the musical bass in the higher register), he is usually attempting to represent innocence.[41] That this is also the case here is demonstrated by the ascending figure to 'macht mir den Himmel auf'. It signifies that the death of Christ has restored us to a state of innocence. However, the two continuo passages, the first of which is as follows (bb. 116 ff.)

are without doubt a depiction of the entombment of Christ. They thus have a function similar to the interjections 'Ruhet sanfte, ruhet wohl!' of the second choir in section B of the final chorus of the St Matthew Passion (in which cf. bb. 52–4, 57–9, 68–70).

[41] 'Bachs Himmelfahrts-Oratorium', *Bach-Gedenkschrift* (Zurich, 1950), 42–65: at 55–6.

*d. The Arias and Ariosos*

Here again my remarks are based on the version contained in the usual printed editions, and here again Version I (see also *NBA*, appendix 1) differs only with regard to minor details that can be ignored in this context. They are followed by a brief examination of the arias that appeared only in Version II. The movements that occurred only in Version III are no longer extant.

The St John Passion contains eight arias, both in its original and in its final state. Of these three are in the first part, and five in the second. Two of the arias in the second part are preceded by an arioso:

| | |
|---|---|
| 7 | 'Von den Stricken meiner Sünden' (alto) |
| 9 | 'Ich folge dir gleichfalls mit freudigen Schritten' (soprano) |
| 13 | 'Ach, mein Sinn, wo willt du endlich hin' (tenor) |
| 19–20 | 'Betrachte, meine Seel' (bass)—'Erwäge, wie sein blutgefärbter Rücken' (tenor) |
| 24 | 'Eilt, ihr angefochtnen Seelen' (bass and chorus) |
| 30 | 'Es ist vollbracht' (alto) |
| 32 | 'Mein teurer Heiland, laß dich fragen' (bass and chorus) |
| 34–5 | 'Mein Herz, indem die ganze Welt' (tenor)—'Zerfließe, mein Herze' (soprano) |

The soloists' voice types and the instruments employed are both distributed in a strikingly irregular manner. The woodwinds appear only at the start and at the end (nos. 7, 9, 34, 35). No. 32 is a continuo movement, and the other movements are assigned to strings, either tutti (nos. 13, 24, and also 30, 34), violas d'amore (nos. 19, 20; 19 with lute), or viola da gamba (no. 30), whereas the violin—solo or *à due*—is missing entirely. However, no. 9 may originally have been intended for solo violin (see App. I).

We will now examine certain arias in detail and some in a slightly more cursory manner. By and large the formal design employed in the St John Passion does not differ from that used in the cantatas. Of course, Bach took great care over their composition. This is demonstrated, for example, by the virtual disappearance of the pure (or unvaried) da capo form, which occurs only in movement 20.

As an example of this we will examine the first aria, 'Von den Stricken meiner Sünden', in some detail.

The thematic material is displayed in the ritornello (bars 1–8). Despite the concision of the introduction, it is many-sided. Furthermore, Bach varies it continually as the piece progresses. (See also the early version in *NBA*, pp. 191–6.)

To a certain extent the ritornello is modelled on the *Fortspinnung* type, with an antecedent $\alpha$ (bars 1–4), the *Fortspinnung* $\beta$ (bars 5–7) and a concluding cadence (bar 8).

The antecedent consists of a canon for the two oboes ($\alpha$) over a continuo ($\gamma$) in the style of a *basso quasi ostinato* that ascends by steps of a second from d to a and in the process is rhythmically condensed to become figure $\gamma^{I}$ in bar 4. This figure is later used in a variety of ways. In the *Fortspinnung* section there is less polyphony: the *Fortspinnung* pattern is heard in bars 5 (oboe I and II), 6 (oboe I), and 7 (bc), and ends with the cadence. The agitation of the continuo, the motivic character of which is particularly noticeable, initially leads us to construe this as the principal voice—an impression that is reinforced by its almost continual presence in the vocal sections. However, it is not this motif, but canon *α* in the form in which it first appears (oboe II) that is taken up by the voice in section A.

At the start of the first vocal section the ritornello acquires additional text-related significance, for the antithesis of canon and parallel voice-leading obviously corresponds to the concepts of 'binden' and 'entbinden' ('bind' and 'unbind'). This requires some explanation in the first four (canonic) bars, whereas the meaning of the *Fortspinnung* figure *β* is revealed by its repetition together with the words 'mich zu entbinden' (bb. 13, 14, and *passim*).

The leap of a fifth in the canonic figure *α* is subjected to diminution when the beginning of the ritornello is taken up by the voice. Since we are not familiar with this kind of embellishment, it is rather difficult to recognize.

is turned into

Smend (1926: 115) points to the similarity between this figure and the beginning of the aria 'Es ist vollbracht' (movement 30, b. 1, gamba), and sees it as a further example of the interlocking of two movements by means of the identical setting of different texts (cf. the turba choruses). However, it is rather difficult to agree with him. Apart from the fact that, on closer inspection, neither of the two movements helps to emphasize the formal symmetry that Smend presupposes, and that there is also no particular textual correspondence between them,[42] this is not really a case of thematic relationship, but of a link through a diminution figure that in the first example fills a leap of a fifth (see above) and in the second embellishes a linear motion of a fifth (i.e. a stepwise descent, see movement 29, bb. 13–14). Furthermore, in order to bring out the relationship, the figure has to be read from the beginning of the vocal part in movement 7 and from the beginning of the instrumental part in movement 30. Yet the possibility of an intentional reference from movement 30 back to movement 7 cannot be wholly excluded.

The main part of the aria, A (bars 9–38), consists of three vocal sections, a a' a'', which are 8, 8, and 10 bars in length. The first section is separated from the other two, which are contiguous, by an instrumental interlude, so that the impression of bipartite form (the second section being an enlargement of the first) is created. In the course of section A the dependence on the ritornello progressively weakens.

a: The alto begins as a repeat of the oboe II part (bb. 9–12 = 1–4), then jumps to that of oboe I (bb. 13–14 = 5–7), and ends on the dominant (b. 16), whilst the oboes in bars 15–16 take over motif $\gamma'$ from bar 4 of the bc.—Interlude (bb. 17–20 = 5–8).

a': The alto begins as a vocal insert in the ritornello antecedent (bb. 21–4 = 1–4). At the same time the oboes take over the diminution of the head motif from the alto (from b. 9):

turns into

The rest of the section contains a modulation to F, the key of the

[42] The argument is not particularly convincing inasmuch as Bach elsewhere not only assigns musically corresponding passages to sections of text that are similar, but also to sections that are quite different. See Werner Neumann, 'Das Problem "vokal-instrumental" in seiner Bedeutung für ein neues Bach-Verständnis', *Bachforschung und Bachinterpretation heute. Bericht über das Bachfest-Symposium 1978 der Philipps-Universität Marburg* (Kassel, 1981), 72–85.

relative major, in which the fact that bars 25–8 derive from bars 13–16 in the alto (b. 27 = 15 also in the oboes) remains apparent.

a'': Although the links with the ritornello are still clearly perceivable, the connection is less obvious. Cf.
Oboe I and II, bars 29–31 with bars 1–3 (first note of theme an octave lower each time)
Bc, bars 29–31 and Oboe I, bar 32 with Bc, bars 1–4
Alto, bar 33 with bar 13
Alto, bars 35–6 with bars 13–14
etc., while Bach uses the free concluding modulation to the dominant A minor to emphasize the word 'Heil' in contrast to the preceding section (bb. 37–8).

A complete restatement of the ritornello in the dominant (bb. 39–46) leads to section B (bb. 47–65), which is structured with considerably greater freedom. It begins with a modulating section which, with motifs $\gamma$ and $\gamma'$ in the instruments and $\beta$ in the alto, leads first to D minor (b. 54), but then, after three bars (bb. 55–7, which resemble bb. 1–3), moves to the subdominant, G minor, the key that dominates the rest of the middle section. In bars 58–65, which in the instrumental parts turn out to be a very free repeat of the opening ritornello (cf. the bc), there is a gradual return to thematic links, for in the alto bars 62–5 noticeably resemble bars 13–16.

A four-bar instrumental interlude (bb. 66–9) over motif $\beta$, which on this occasion occurs in the bc, brings the middle section to a close.

The reappearance of motif $\alpha'$, which had been banished completely from the middle section, ushers in the free da capo, A', of the main section with a three-bar introduction (bb. 70–2) that is designed to modulate back to the main key of D minor. This corresponds almost exactly to the original section A (bb. 73–86, 90–105 = 9–38). Only bars 87–9 are different. They introduce a subdominant modulation designed to bring the movement to a close in the tonic instead of the dominant.

The repetition of the opening ritornello (bb. 106–14 = 1–9$^{a}$) brings the movement to an end.

As in the case of this aria, the ones that follow are noticeably influenced by the text, though, as we shall see, in a variety of different ways.

In the aria 'Ich folge dir gleichfalls mit freudigen Schritten', it is initially, as one might expect, the idea of the follower which determines the musical image. The figure of mimesis or *fuga* (which theorists often do not distinguish precisely) becomes an emblem of *imitatio Christi*, the imitation of Christ, either in the shape of self-imitation (bb. 1–2),

as an (intervallic) sequence (bb. 5–8),

or as a canon (bb. 16–20).

But in the middle section, B (b b' in formal terms), Bach develops new images, first the *gradatio* (bb. 61–4)

and then, during the repeat in b', the *exclamatio* (bb. 86–9).

In the aria 'Ach, mein Sinn' Bach was faced with the task of setting a text that had originally been written for an *intrada* by Sebastian Knüpfer, and which for this reason, with its eleven lines, was rather long (see above, p. 43; Weise prints the text as an eight-line poem with internal rhymes). He thus eschews any kind of reference back to the beginning of the text in the vocal part and creates a tripartite sequence:

A 'Ach, mein Sinn' (bb. 17–45)
B 'Bleib ich hier' (bb. 47–59)
C 'Bei der Welt' (bb. 63–89)

The instrumental ritornello in sarabande rhythm[43] begins over a chromatically descending *lamento* bass. The upper voice (violin I) of bars 1–8 was evidently composed for the beginning of the text and for this reason is repeated in section A by the tenor together with violin I. The second half of the ritornello consists of a purely instrumental *Fortspinnung* (a sequence of 2 + 2 + 1 + 1 bars) and the final cadence.

In this aria the formal cohesion that the tenor voice is unable to provide on account of the changing nature of the text is ensured by the instrumental writing, and this may well be the reason why Bach at first wanted it to be played with 'tutti li Stromenti' before deciding to exclude the woodwinds (see below, p. 111). In fact, Bach rarely constructed an aria almost completely on the basis of repeated instrumental ritornellos,[44] as he did here, where he introduced wholly different vocal lines which took their bearings from the text.

The aria 'Erwäge, wie sein blutgefärbter Rücken' is particularly rich in imagery. The individual motifs, which a theorist would probably subsume under the term *hypotyposis* figures (figures of depiction), illustrate careful consideration (b. 1[a]):

the watery billows (b. 22[b]):

[43] See *TBSt* 6, pp. 62–4.
[44] Bb. 17–24 = 1–8; 32–46 = 1–5; 52–62 = 1–11; 63–73 = 1–11; 74–88 = 1–15; 89–91 = 26–8. Also cf. bc in bb. 47–9 = 1–3.

and the rainbow (b. $25^b$):

to name but the most important ones.

In the aria 'Eilt, ihr angefochtnen Seelen' (movement 24) the figure of the ascending scale is immediately understood as an image of haste. This is complemented by the questions 'Where to?' ('Wohin?') of the 'souls that are tempted' ('angefochtnen Seelen') in the form of ascending intervallic leaps which Bach compressed into 2/8 rhythm within the 3/8 metre,[45] thereby showing the questioners' lack of orientation. The leaps are particularly conspicuous in combination with the concept of 'Marterhöhlen', which are depicted by means of chromaticism, altered thirds, and a broken diminished seventh chord (bb. 42–6):

(Violin II, viola, and bc have been omitted in this example)

As we have seen, in the aria 'Es ist vollbracht' Bach refers to the preceding words of Jesus as related by St John, which were set to music as follows (movement 29, bb. 13–14):

[45] See Peter Böttinger, 'aus dem tact gerathen', in Heinz-Klaus Metzger and Rainer Riehn (eds.), *Johann Sebastian Bach: Die Passionen* (Musik-Konzepte 50/51) (Edition text + kritik, Munich, 1986), 117–20.

The musical rendering of this utterance is full of variety. Whereas the figure is presented largely unaltered in rhythmic terms, namely ♪♪♫♪♪ or in embellished form ♬♪♪♬♪♪, it occurs (after the recitative version above) in the aria as follows.

Here is the entry in the viola da gamba (b. 1):

This figure is then repeated on several scale degrees.

When the alto enters, it is repeated twice in succession, first a fourth higher, and then as in the entry of the viola da gamba, though with an octave leap after the initial note (bb. 5–6):

In the final section of the aria, after the words 'und schließt den Kampf', the figure, in keeping with the character of an ending, returns to the version of the recitative (movement 29), although it is transposed from F♯ minor to B minor (b. 40):

The middle section of the aria contains another interesting figure, the melisma to the word 'Kampf' that occurs in bb. 30–1:

It may of course simply be a coincidence, but the allusion to the figuration in the opening chorus which embellishes the words 'Herrscher' and 'herrlich' is clearly audible.

In keeping with the text, Bach based this aria on formal contrast. Section A, marked 'Molt' adagio', is followed by section B, marked 'vivace', and this in turn is followed by a brief recapitulation of the opening section, which should be termed coda rather than A'. The contrast between the opening and the middle sections extends to virtually every aspect of the piece.

[Contrast between sections A and B in the aria 'Es ist vollbracht']

| | A | B |
|---|---|---|
| Scoring | with solo gamba | with tutti strings |
| Time signature | 4/4 | 3/4 |
| Mode | minor | major |
| Harmonic style | complex | simple |
| Rhythm | differentiated | uniform |
| | dotted | flowing |
| Melodic style | small range | large range |
| | vocal | instrumental |
| | stepwise | broken chords |
| | text-based, declamatory | repeated notes |

The extent to which such contrasts are prefigured in the thinking of the fourth evangelist is demonstrated by sayings such as 'And the light shineth in the darkness' (John 1: 5) or 'In the world ye shall have tribulation: but be of good cheer: I have overcome the world' (John 16: 33).

Separated from this by only a single bar of the Evangelist ('Und neiget das Haupt und verschied') and an ensuing cadence, there follows the next aria, 'Mein teurer Heiland, laß dich fragen'. Here the text once again refers to the last words of Jesus. However, the poet and the composer do their best to suppress any impression of redundancy.

Our attention shifts from Jesus, who is victorious in death, to the congregation, whom he has redeemed by dying. It is represented by the chorus which sings the chorale. Despite the words that precede it, 'und verschied' ('and gave up the ghost'), the aria has the character of a festive dance in a major key,[46] which is overlapped by the steady progress of the chorale. Furthermore, it is not necessary to adduce a great deal of evidence in order to demonstrate that the vocal melody, despite its loving attention to the details of the text,[47] is fundamentally instrumental

[46] That the major melody of the chorale would not have prevented Bach from writing the aria in the minor is demonstrated by movement 11⁺ of Version II.

[47] Cf. esp. the lower chromatic alteration on 'Sterben' (bb. 14, 16), on 'Pein' (b. 21) and on 'Schmerzen' (b. 33), the diminished seventh after 'Schmerzen' (bar 31), and the *exclamatio* on 'ja' (bb. 37–8).

in character, so that—for the first time in this Passion—it is possible to call into question whether the opening ritornello was in fact devised with the words of the text which follows in mind. The primacy of instrumental invention is apparent, for example, in the syncopated accent on the word 'Hei-lánd' (with *tr*!) in bar 3, in the differing text underlay of musically identical (or similar) passages (cf. b. 3 with bb. 9 and 41–2, b. 14 with b. 24, or b. 10[a] with b. 10[b]), and in the large size of the intervals, which are not absolutely necessary from a textual point of view. They might possibly constitute an image of the freedom of those who have been delivered from death (cf. b. 14: 'frei', b. 22: 'Himmelreich', bar 24: 'Erlösung'), though they could equally well depict their joy.

The connection with the chorale text is immediately apparent. However, this is true only in general terms. It is difficult to point to specific similarities such as those found in movement 11⁺ (see p. 48).

In formal terms this is an aria over a *basso quasi ostinato* whose overall design is determined by that of the chorale.

The final aria of the Passion, 'Zerfließe, mein Herze', only makes sense in conjunction with the interpolation from St Matthew (movement 33), and was thus removed together with the latter in Version III.

The motivic material presented in the opening ritornello predominates throughout the movement. The beginning introduces a syncopated motif $\alpha$, a demisemiquaver figure $\beta$, and a pounding motif $\gamma$ (bb. 1–2):

In bb. 9–11 a staccato motif $\delta$ then appears:

$\alpha$ is presumably intended to depict fright, $\beta$ melting, and $\gamma$ the beating[48] of the heart, whereas $\delta$ depicts teardrops.

The vocal part begins with figure $\alpha$, whereas the continuation is largely free. On the other hand, the motifs in the instrumental parts referred to above are almost omnipresent, even during the vocal sections.

Section A begins with a 'motto' (i.e. an anticipation of the first line, bb. 17–20). The main section proper comprises segment a (bb. 25–38), which ends with a vocal insert in the first half of the ritornello (bb. 33–40 = 1–8). This is followed by a shortened segment a' (bars 41–50) and, as an interlude, the second half of the ritornello (bb. 51–8 = 9–16).

The middle section B is particularly impressive; here again an initial segment, b, is followed by a shorter one, c. Bach's art is revealed in the increasingly free treatment of the voice part. It begins with unmistakable allusions to a (cf. b. 59 with b. 25; bb. 61, 65, and 69 with b. 47; bb. 63–4 with bb. 25–6), and subsequently finds wholly new and highly expressive ways of rendering the word 'tot': the descending leap of a sixth (b. 70, also bb. 83–4), the suspended second (bb. 73, 84, 85, 88), the use of *Bebung* (vibrato or tremolo) on chromatically descending held notes (bb. 80–2),[49] and the particularly expressive tritonal progression a' f' e♭' (b. 82).

The free da capo A' begins as a recapitulation of section A (bb. 97–107 = 17–29; bb. 23–4 are omitted), though from bar 108 onwards it moves to the subdominant in order to facilitate the ending on the tonic (bb. 108–18 = 30–40). However, the shortened segment a' of section A is completely recast in A', so that the vocal insert in bars 1–8 from A (in A': bb. 111–18) is also followed by the remaining bars of the ritornello, at first with a vocal insert (bb. 119–22 = 9–12), and then, after a vocal cadence (bar 123), as an epilogue (bb. 124–7 = 13–16).

Two arias in the Passion are linked to the arioso movements that immediately precede them, namely movements 20 and 35 to movements 19 and 34—a phenomenon with which the modern listener is familiar from the St Matthew Passion, where such ariosos are termed 'Recitativo'

[48] Repeated notes supplied with a slur are nowadays usually taken to signify bow vibrato. See Greta Moens-Haenen, *Das Vibrato in der Musik des Barock* (Graz, 1988). However, similar figures also occur in the woodwind parts (e.g. bb. 17–19, 43–5, and elsewhere).

[49] Greta Moens-Haenen, 'Zur Frage der Wellenlinien in der Musik Johann Sebastian Bachs', *Archiv für Musikwissenschaft*, 41 (1984), 176–86, contends that this signifies a glissando *Bebung*. However, this has not gone unchallenged. See Josef Rainerius Fuchs, 'Halbtonglissando und Orgeltremulantimitation in Bachs Musik?', *Mf* 43 (1990), 247–52.

and where they play a much larger role. The original reason for their insertion may have been the classification into reading, meditation upon what has been read, and final prayer, which was familiar from instructions on how to read the Bible.[50] In the context of a Passion composition, 'reading' is assigned to what is sung by the Evangelist and the speaking characters, 'meditation' to the arioso, and 'prayer' to the aria. In the St John Passion this tripartite division is seen at the most in movements 33 to 35 (inasmuch as one is prepared to construe 'Zerfließe, mein Herze' as a prayer), whereas it is difficult to perceive a similar differentiation in the pair of movements 19–20, 'Betrachte'–'Erwäge', which follow on the report of the scourging of Jesus.

The contrast between the function of the two pairs of movements also becomes clearly evident in the musical composition. 'Betrachte'–'Erwäge' form a homogeneous unit that already finds expression in the refined choice of solo instruments. However, in the arioso the two violas d'amore, which are common to both movements, merely form the background sonority for the figuration of the lute, which is used only in this movement of the St John Passion,[51] and which imparts to it an unmistakable shading. It ushers in the kind of 'motivically enhanced *accompagnato*' (Werner Neumann) with which we are familiar from the St Matthew Passion and also from some of Bach's cantatas. Thus we may tentatively repeat Schering's conjecture (*KM*, 77 n. 1) that the contrast between the plucked broken chords of the lute and the vocal melodic style of the viola d'amore, which proceeds mainly by intervals of a second, was inspired by the textual contrast between 'thorns, the which do pierce him' ('Dornen, so ihn stechen') and 'Heaven's primroses' ('Himmelsschlüsselblumen'). In addition to the attractive quality of the instrumentation we must emphasize that of the vocal declamation generated by the text, and underpinned by richly expressive harmony such as the diminished seventh (with the bc) on 'ängstlichem' (b. 3) and 'Jesu Schmerzen' (bb. 6–7), the tritone leap on 'mit bittrer' (b. 4) and 'so ihn stechen' (b. 8), the minor ninth (with the bc) on 'halb beklemmtem' (b. 5), the triadic melody on 'dein höchstes Gut' (bb. 5–6) and 'Himmelsschlüsselblumen' (b. 9), but also on 'ohn Unterlaß' (b. 15); and finally the various ways of setting the words 'auf ihn', some of which emphasize the word 'ihn' by means of wide ascending intervals (bb. 12,

[50] See Martin Dibelius, 'Individualismus und Gemeindebewußtsein in Joh. Seb. Bachs Passionen', *Archiv für Reformationsgeschichte*, 41 (1948), repr. in id., *Botschaft und Geschichte*, i (Tübingen, 1953).

[51] Replaced by the organ or harpsichord in later performances, just as the violas d'amore were replaced by muted violins, doubtless only as a makeshift measure.

13), though sometimes quite differently, i.e. with a suspended second (bb. 14, 16). Furthermore, a number of reminiscences and allusions, the significance of which should of course not be overestimated, make for a certain motivic cohesion (initially the movement sounds rather improvisatory), for example, the leaps of a seventh on 'Betrachte' (b. 2), 'mit ängstlichem' (b. 3), 'von seiner Wermut' (bb. 10–11), 'auf ihn' (b. 13); the descending intervals on 'wie dir' (b. 7) and 'drum sieh' (bb. 11–12); and the descending triad in bb. 9 and 15 that has already been mentioned above.

The connection between the second arioso (movement 34) and the aria that follows is rather different. Whereas the *soteriological* significance of Jesus's sufferings was at the centre of movement 19, movement 34 once more dwells on the *events* reported earlier. In the strings we again hear the earth quaking, the veil of the temple being rent in twain, the rocks being rent, and the graves being opened. Only in the penultimate bar do we hear a sigh and *Bebung* (bow vibrato) figure as an answer to the question of the Christian's response to these events. The key relationships are also revealing: whereas movements 19–20 have E♭ major – C minor, movements 34–5 have G major – C major – F minor. In terms of keys, the final section of the Passion begins with movement 35!

Let us briefly consider the three arias that occur only in Version II. One is immediately struck by the unusually dramatic quality of two of the three movements, though there may be various reasons for this.

As is revealed by the text (see above, p. 48), movement 11⁺, the aria 'Himmel reiße, Welt erbebe', was, it seems, originally destined for a later place in the Passion narrative, and not as a meditation on the fact that one of the officers had struck Jesus with the palm of his hand, a relatively harmless occurrence. If the aria comes from a Passion at all, it can only have been intended for a place in the immediate vicinity of the death of Jesus, where its dramatic quality would be perfectly comprehensible. The subtle combination of the free poetry of the text and the chorale strophe sung by the soprano has already been pointed out. It is a relationship for which there is no parallel in Bach's extant works.

In compositional terms this is an aria over a *basso quasi ostinato*. It is decidedly baroque in character, and the overall formal design is to a large extent determined by the chorale. The role of the two transverse flutes is of secondary importance. They merely serve to enhance the overall sonority, and we will not go far wrong if we assume that Bach added them only when the movement was incorporated in the St John Passion in 1725.[52]

Various unusual features suggest that the movement went through a number of stages. For example, the head motif of b. 1 occurs twice with the sixth as fourth note (in bb. 1 and 7), and thereafter only with the octave: bb. 12, (16), 29, 50, 55. Did the beginning originally sound like this?

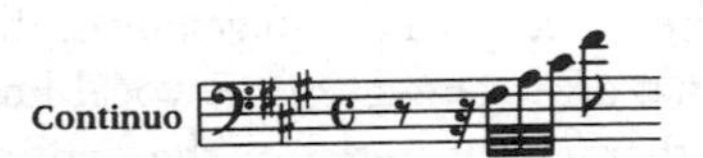


And was the movement originally in the key of E minor (choir pitch),[53] so that Bach, when transposing the part to F♯ minor, wished to spare the continuo basses the rather high f♯'? The figure that first occurs in bar 5

(and in bb. 20, 25–6) is occasionally given a tied note instead of a rest (for example, in bb. 14, 23, 40, 41, 43), though this discrepancy may simply be the chance result of a process of compositional development.

That the sixth line of the chorale (bb. 36–7) also points to the earlier origins of the aria has already been noted above (p. 6).

The formal design of the aria is determined by the length of the text, which has sixteen lines. These in turn are related to the eight lines of the chorale, and in such a way that each pair of lines of free poetry is followed by a line of the chorale.[54] The vocal part is non-thematic (with a few motivic similarities; for example, cf. b. 8 with bb. 20, 40, 41; bb. 29–30 and 30–1 with bb. 33, 49, 50) and follows the text with appropriate figures:

[52] This may be corroborated by the fact that Bach still notates the characteristic rhythm of the flutes ♪♩ ♬ as ♫♫ when it first appears in bar 11 (fltr 1). Perhaps he decided to use it (frequently) only as the work progressed.

[53] Some of the corrections in the original parts seem to suggest that this was so. See Mendel, *KB*, pp. 327–8, on bb. 17 (basso), 26, 34, 55, to some extent 17 (fltr I), and 19. Other emendations may be put down to the general insecurity of the scribe who transposed the piece.

[54] The rhyme scheme also follows that of the chorale verse, and this leads to a fairly complicated verse structure. The odd lines of the aria text do not rhyme, whereas the even lines rhyme with the following line of the chorale.

B. 8 'Erbebe': broken triads
Bb. 17–18 'Schmerzen': chromaticism
Bb. 29–30 'Kreuzeswegen': cruciform figures
Bb. 38–9 'Sterben': chromaticism, diminished seventh leaps (allusions to the B minor fugue, *Well-Tempered Clavier I*, BWV 869/2)

Bach provides a caesura within the otherwise continuous singing of the bass only between the *Stollen* and the *Abgesang* of the chorale, bb. 27–8.

In view of the serial arrangement of the vocal lines, formal cohesion is provided by the thematic material of the continuo, which, though often varied, is none the less always seen to derive from the opening ritornello.

Movement $13^{II}$, the aria 'Zerschmettert mich, ihr Felsen und ihr Hügel', is one of the few compositions by Bach that his contemporaries may rightly have termed 'operatic'. Its dramatic character is obvious. Yet however delightful the demisemiquaver runs inspired by the word 'Strahl'; however impressive the alternation between strict (aria) and free (recitative) tempo, which renders the shift from visible events to inner remorse; however successful and indeed exemplary the Neapolitan sixth on 'Jesu' introduced in b. 26 in order to highlight the word: the aria cannot be considered an improvement on 'Ach, mein Sinn'. At the most it would occasionally make a welcome change.

Similarly, the aria 'Ach windet euch nicht so, geplagte Seelen' (movement $19^{II}$) was inserted in place of 'Betrachte'–'Erwäge' (movements 19–20) not because the composer wished to replace the latter with something that was less imperfect. In fact, the scoring for two oboes repeats that of the aria 'Von den Stricken meiner Sünden' and is thus less interesting than that of the movements which were its predecessors in the Passion. Furthermore, the constricted range of motifs $\alpha$ and $\beta$ which determine the movement's thematic material (initially in oboe I, bb. 1 and 3)—

of which the first depicts writhing, and the second the fear and suffering of the cross—is not on a par with the rich expressivity of the arioso 'Betrachte, meine Seel', even though Bach manages to combine the motifs in remarkable manner,[55] and even though the climax of the movement with the stretto (bb. 61–2) and inversion (b. 65) of motif $\beta$ must certainly command admiration. The fact that, despite the reference to section A in section B (see n. 55, above), there is a complete da capo of bb. 1–42, results from the need to return to the main key, C minor.

## 4. PROBLEMS ASSOCIATED WITH THE OVERALL FORMAL DESIGN AND THE DIFFERENT VERSIONS

Ever since the overall formal design of the St John Passion began to be seen to possess a special significance as a result of Friedrich Smend's pioneering analysis in *BJ* (1926) it has been described as symmetrical, or as 'chiastic-cyclic'. Werner Breig (1985: 65, 90–4) has narrowed down this reading considerably, whereas an explication of the sequence of keys (most recently in Chafe (1981) ) seems to confirm Smend's views and not to contradict them. I will briefly describe the most important formal interpretations that have been postulated so far, and, in the ensuing critical appraisal, attempt to define my own views on the matter. As we shall see, I am largely in agreement with Breig.

First, however, some basic remarks. (The reader is also referred to App. IV, 'The Problem of Symmetry in Bach's Work'.)

The oratorio Passion differs from the cantata and even from the Mass in that it is based on a connected biblical narrative that is both presented and commented upon. Thus whereas in a cantata such as the 'Actus Tragicus' (BWV 106) the textual design can arbitrarily place a climax at a point where the subject matter makes it seem particularly appropriate (in our example at the centre of the cantata through the simultaneous interpretation of death as necessity and as the desired union with Jesus), the emphasis within the Passion remains dependent on the biblical narrative, in other words, on an account that on the whole moves straight towards the Crucifixion. By and large the form of

[55] At its very first occurrence (b. 3) $\beta$ is combined with a variant of $\alpha$. The *Fortspinnung* (bb. 5–8) consists of a two-bar extension of $\alpha$, and the ritornello coda (b. 9) is derived from bar 3. The beginning of section A has a vocal version of bb. 1–2 (bb. 11–12, motto) and a vocal and instrumental repeat of bb. 1–10 (in bb. 17–26), and section B also has sophisticated references to the opening ritornello (cf. bb. 45–50 with bb. 5–10, and bb. 59–60 with bb. 1–2) and to section A (cf. bb. 69–72 with bb. 27–30).

the latter also determines the musical design: at most it permits certain nuances of emphasis, but no real rearrangement. For this reason Breig believes that the correspondences perceived in the turba choruses have been exaggerated, 'for they make it difficult to do full justice to the unique and specific textual situation in musical terms' (1985: 87).

Smend's analysis of 1926 is based on the premiss that it was the task of the turba choruses, more than that of the other movements of the Passion, to define and establish the form of the work:

Only the dramatic choruses are common to all the extant versions . . . If Bach . . . had noticed something that needed to be improved in the form of the dramatic choruses, he would certainly have made changes here as well. That he did not do so suggests (even before we have studied them in detail) that they are of crucial importance for the overall structure, indeed, that it is precisely their interrelationships which reveal the ground plan. (p. 107)

In what follows Smend examines a series of correspondences which primarily involve the turba choruses, but also other movements, for example, the motivic relationship between aria movements 7 and 30 mentioned above, or the 'aria–short recitative–aria' sequence in movements 7–9 and 30–32. However, in the final analysis only the sequence of movements termed 'Herzstück' (centrepiece) turns out to be a convincing symmetrical construct, as is demonstrated by the following design suggested by Smend [see p. 97].[56]

Smend believed that the logic of the symmetrical design derived from the subject matter of the Passion:

Many listeners must have sensed that the chorale 'Durch dein Gefängnis' [22] is one of the supreme moments of the whole Passion . . . And this chorale turns out to be the centre of the whole work, and its climax. Prior to this the action ascends, and from this point on it descends. Before the chorale Pilate is prepared not to put Jesus to death, for he is convinced of his innocence. Thereafter he yields step by step to the pressure of the crowd. Modern listeners might perhaps assign the climax of a passion to the death of Jesus. However, if we approach the St John Passion with the preconceived idea that Bach ought to follow suit in this regard, and if we look for the climax in the Golgotha scene, we will perhaps be disappointed by movements such as the chorus 'Lasset uns den nicht zerteilen' [27$^{b}$]. Here he elaborates something that is of secondary importance in too much detail. Furthermore, the aria and chorale, 'Mein teurer Heiland' [32], may not altogether satisfy our expectations. Everything at this point is rather weak compared with what has already been heard in earlier parts of the work. However, as

[56] In the following the numbers of movements used in the older literature have been replaced by those of the *NBA* (in square brackets).

soon as we have understood the architecture, we know that by this time the climax is a long way behind us, and that the work is approaching its end. (pp. 120–1)

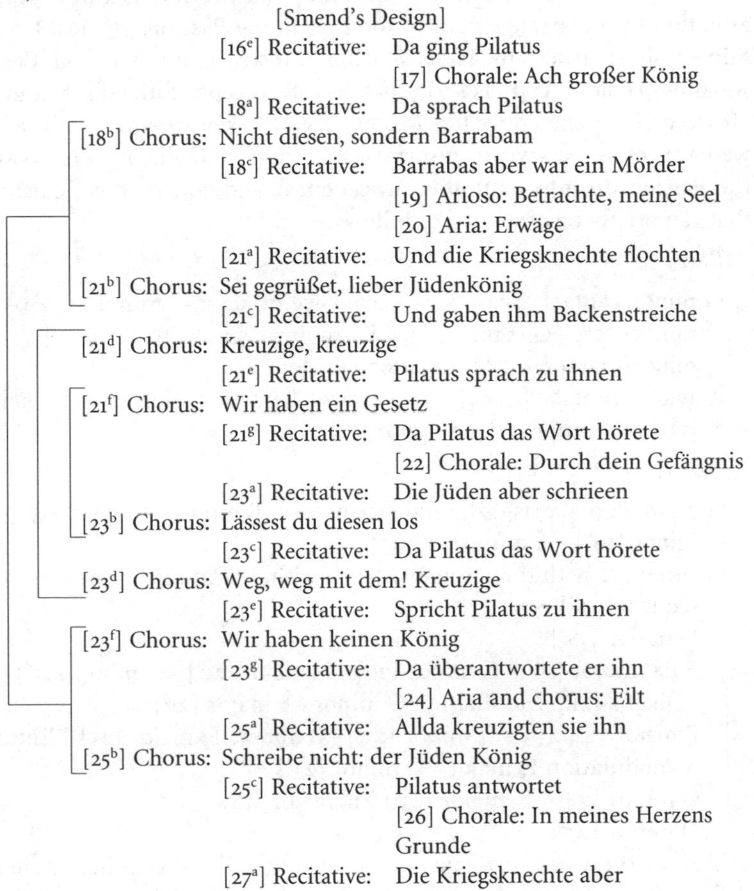


Smend's contention that 'the death of Jesus' does not constitute a climax in Bach's Passion is of course not altogether convincing. The casting of lots for the garment is not closely connected with the account of the death of Jesus. Smend ought not to have mentioned chorus $27^b$ at this juncture. That he does so none the less is due to his basic premiss, the idea of the formal function of the turba choruses. He fails to explain why the aria 'Mein teurer Heiland' does not altogether satisfy our expectations. And to prove that the arias 'Es ist vollbracht' or 'Zerfließe, mein Herze' are less 'supreme moments of the whole Passion' than 'Durch dein Gefängnis' would not be easy, even for someone like Smend (should he have attempted to do so).

Shortly after Smend's important study, Bach scholars turned their attention to the arrangement of the keys in the Passion. *BJ* (1932) contains a short article by Hans Joachim Moser, 'Zum Bau von Bachs Johannespassion' (pp. 155–7), that largely accepts Smend's findings. However, over and above this Moser suggests a key scheme which (after we have corrected several misprints) is certainly convincing. He divides the Passion up into a number of 'cantatas', and comes to conclusions that can briefly be described as follows:[57]

Part I

G minor cantata [1–10, b. 15], sequence of keys: G minor [1, $2^b$] – C minor [$2^d$] – G minor [3] – D minor [5, 7] – B♭ major [9] – G minor/major [10]. Modulation [10] to:

A major cantata [11–14], sequence of keys: A major [11] – E major [$12^b$] – F♯ minor [13] – A major [14].

Part II

A minor cantata [15–17], sequence of keys: E minor/Phrygian [15] – D minor [$16^b$] – A minor [$16^d$, 17].

Centrepiece with three tonality levels within D minor frame [18–$27^a$], sequence of keys:

D minor [$18^b$]

E flat major [19] – C minor [20] – B♭ major [$21^b$] – G minor [$21^d$] – F major [$21^f$]. Modulation G minor – E major [$21^g$]

E major [22, $23^b$] – F♯ minor [$23^d$] – B minor/ F♯ major [23 f]. Return modulation F♯ major – G minor [$23^g$]

G minor [24] – B♭ major [$25^b$] – E♭ major [26]

D minor [$27^a$]

'Rest of the work' [$27^b$–39; 40 not mentioned], descending circle of fifths framed by movements in C major [$27^b$] and C minor [39]: A major [28] – B minor [30] – D major [32] – G/C major [34] – F minor [35, 37].

Moser subsequently attempted to prove that the chorale melodies also contribute to the formal design, though here the conclusions he reaches are less convincing.

It is certainly possible to point to weaker aspects of Moser's interpretation, for example, the occasional and illogical inclusion of some of the recitatives, or the description of the fairly numerous and important

[57] Moser largely disregards the (modulating) recitatives.

movements 27$^{b}$–39 as the 'rest of the work'—a phrase that smacks of Smend's way of thinking—not to mention the omission of movement 40 in the key scheme.[58] And the supposed correspondence between movements 27$^{b}$ and 39 is rather irritating (see n. 55, above). However, the place of the C major movement 27$^{b}$ also proves to be problematical in the case of the two interpretations referred to below. All in all, however, Moser's interpretation could have served as a useful starting-point if it had become more widely known.

In *Musik und Kirche*, 40 (1970: 33), Dieter Weiss published a short (and thus rather lucid) interpretation of the key scheme. He omits the recitatives (because they modulate), and arrives at groups 'which tend towards a central key'. One movement always represents 'the typical central key'. The result may be summarized as follows:

[Weiss's interpretation of the key scheme]

| Part | Movements | Typical key (movt) | Sequence of keys |
|---|---|---|---|
| I | 1–3 | G min (1) | G min G min C min G min |
| | 5–9 | D min (5) | D min D min B♭maj |
| II | 11–14 | A maj (11) | A maj A maj [or E maj?] F♯ min A maj |
| | 15–18$^{b}$ | A min (17) | E min/Phrygian D min A min A min D min |
| | 19–21$^{f}$ | B♭maj (21$^{b}$) | E♭maj C min B♭maj G min F maj |
| | 22–23$^{f}$ | E maj (22) | E maj E maj F♯ min B min |
| | 24–27$^{b}$ | E♭maj (26) | G min B♭maj E♭maj C maj |
| | 28–34 | D maj (32) | A maj B min/D maj D maj G maj |
| | 35–40 | C min (39) | F min F min C min E♭maj |

Here Moser's G minor cantata and what he refers to as the 'rest of the work' are each divided into two groups, and the 'centrepiece' into three groups. The delimitation of the key areas sometimes deviates from that of Moser, though not significantly.

The most recent interpretation of the key scheme is the one put forward by Eric Chafe (1981 and 1988). He goes back to Smend's idea that the symmetrical form is an allegorical reference to the cross of Jesus, and believes that the same kind of symmetry can be discerned in the key scheme. In this he largely follows the pattern devised by Dieter Weiss,[59] though he joins up the latter's groups 1 and 2 (as does Moser), and

[58] A result of confusing parallel and relative keys. The C minor of movement 39, by being related to the C major of movement 27$^{b}$, is no longer available for the E♭ of movement 40.

[59] However, he quotes Weiss only in order to criticize him, namely with regard to movement 27$^{b}$. He refers to Moser in a similar way.

creates a separate group for movement $27^{b}$, so that we are again left with a total of nine.

The new feature of Chafe's approach is the fact that his groups are based on sharp keys, flat keys, and keys without key signatures (natural keys). By eschewing any further subdivisions, he is able to suggest a large-scale plan that at first sight appears to be a decidedly symmetrical arrangement. Furthermore, the symmetry not only extends to the 'centrepiece', but to the Passion as a whole.

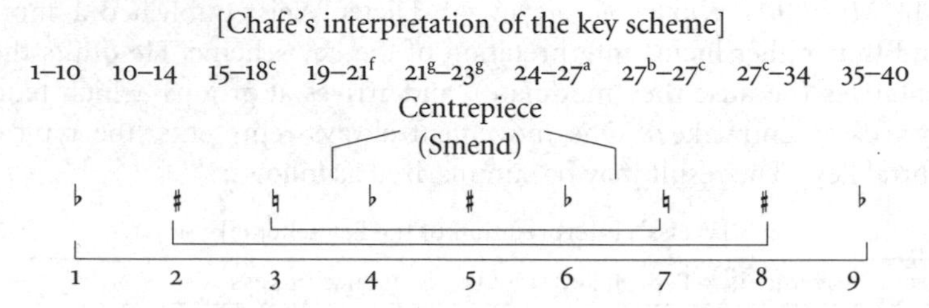


But several problems become apparent when one examines this scheme more closely. In particular there is the question of whether such a formalistic interpretation of the key scheme can possibly correspond to Bach's intentions. For it presupposes that the composer chose to ignore natural relationships, preferring instead to interpret a modulation from G to C as a shift to a new key, and one from G to C♯ as evidence of a single key. Is it permissible to imply that this was Bach's understanding of tonality?

It is also necessary to call into question the two ♮ groups. The first, group 3, contains two movements in D minor ($16^{b}$ $18^{b}$), which can be interpreted as ♮ movements only because Bach, in keeping with tradition, notated them without an accidental ('Dorian'). But if this is so, then Chafe ought not to include movements 10 and $27^{c}$ as sharp keys, for to the very end they do not have key signatures either. Even more problematical is the definition of a chorus, 'Lasset uns den nicht zerteilen', and the two bars of recitative, $27^{b}$–$27^{c}$, that follow (the third bar already begins to modulate!) as a self-contained 'group'. This is of particular importance to Chafe, for he makes polemical remarks about Moser and Weiss, who interpret this differently. However, this division creates disproportions which suggest a symmetry that merely exists on paper. And finally, Smend, as we have seen (p. 97) does not begin the 'centrepiece' with movement 19, but with movement $16^{e}$ (bar 63), which is in the middle of Chafe's ♮ area. Here again the diagram suggests a conformity that does not in fact exist.

Thus at the most we might accept Chafe's symmetrical scheme 'as a useful abbreviation of the real relationships' (Breig), and must call into question whether Bach allowed himself to be guided by such an inartistic and mechanical understanding of keys in the planning of the work.[60]

If we cast our minds back to the division of the passion narrative into five *actus* (pp. 51–2), we will discover no direct parallels to the perceived formal or tonal correspondences, apart from the fact that each *actus* ends with a chorale. True, the 'centrepiece' (as described by Smend) also forms the centre of the middle and third *actus*, 'Pilatus'. However, the grouping of the outer sections and the way *actus* 3 is marked off from them is neither confirmed nor called into question by the referential system of the turba choruses.

Such considerations should form the basis of a critique of the various formal analyses that starts out from the fact that it is impossible to discern any kind of congruity between the narrative, formal, and tonal orders. In brief, the main points are as follows:

> Narrative (division into five *actus*): unequal segments; symmetry of the turba choruses only in 'Pilatus'; tonal grouping not congruent with the *actus* 'Pontifices', 'Pilatus', and 'Crux'.
>
> Form: The referential system of the turba choruses does not cover the entire action; corresponding movements are in contrary tonal areas;[61] the two symmetries do not coincide (Chafe's interpretation glosses over this fact).
>
> Key scheme: the various interpretations merely suggest approximate solutions.

The possibility of arriving at different interpretations speaks in favour

[60] Chafe (1988) also emphasizes the fact that Bach's Passion adheres closely to the theology of St John's Gospel, though, unlike Breig, continues to give credence to the fundamental significance of formal symmetry for an interpretation of the work. It is possible to learn much from this perceptive study even if one finds it impossible to agree with all Chafe says. Thus it must remain an open question whether the incongruity between Smend's 'centrepiece' and Chafe's key scheme (see also n. 61) casts doubt on the proposed symmetrical design of the Passion. This applies to an even greater extent to the supposed symmetry of the Gospel report of Pilate's interrogation, which, though perhaps unnoticed by St John, was 'undoubtedly' discovered by Bach. According to Chafe it was this which prompted Bach to arrange the centrepiece in a symmetrical manner. However, it coincides neither with the symmetry of the centrepiece nor with that of the key scheme.

[61] Movement $18^{b}$: ♮ area–$23^{f}$: ♯ area
Movement $21^{d}$: ♭ area–$23^{d}$: ♯ area
Movement $21^{f}$: ♭ area–$23^{b}$: ♯ area
See Breig (1985: 93–4).

of and not against the stature of a work of art. Thus it would be wrong to treat the incongruity of the different interpretations of the work as a shortcoming that is the fault of musicologists or even of the composer.[62]

However, the large number of interpretations (to which others that have not been discussed here could easily be added) does not absolve us from the duty to ask whether Bach really intended to create a musically determined system of order that went beyond the unfolding of the Passion movement by movement, and if so, whether this was designed to exist without reference to the listener, or was to be perceived by him. If the former were true, then Bach was obviously convinced that an order that the listener cannot perceive is unconsciously felt to have artistic value (as, for example, in the case of serial music), whereas if the latter were true, the order would have been created in the expectation that attentive listeners would be able to hear it.

Since Bach never referred to the matter, it is virtually impossible to give a precise answer. However, it is legitimate to ask which of the orders observed in the notated music of the St John Passion can in fact be perceived by the listener. They obviously include the narration of the events which lead from the moment when Jesus is arrested to his death and burial, the associated contemplative movements, and also the correspondence of the turba choruses—as soon as the second of several corresponding choruses is heard. Thus the listener will understand that movements $2^b$ and $2^d$ constitute a pair after he has heard movement $2^d$. The same is true of movements $16^b$ and $16^d$ after $16^d$, and of movements $16^d$ and $18^b$ (which are related to $2^b$, $2^d$) after $18^b$. In contrast to this he will initially perceive $21^b$, $21^d$, and $21^f$ as single movements, and then, when $23^b$ is played, note the existence of another pair of movements (in analogy to $16^b + 16^d$), and subsequently be reminded of $21^d$ in movement $23^d$, of $2^b$, $2^d$, $16^d$, and $18^b$ in movement $23^f$, and of $21^b$ in movement $25^b$. In other words, even the most attentive listener at first perceives only pairs and groups of movements. In contrast to this, he will perceive the symmetry of the 'centrepiece' only at a later stage, especially in view of the fact that additional features obscure the true state of affairs:

(a) The identity of the 'Kreuzige' choruses, which reminds the listener of the 'Jesum von Nazareth' choruses $2^b$ and $2^d$, is considered to be natural and even self-evident. It is not felt to constitute a special symmetry.

[62] Rather, the confusion is caused by the misguided enthusiasm of certain scholars, who, flying in the face of the evidence, are concerned to make their ideas of symmetry coincide with those of Smend (see also n. 61, above).

(b) The same is true of the 'Jüdenkönig' choruses $21^{b}$ and $25^{b}$.
(c) The choruses referred to under (a) and (b) occur at points that are predetermined by the text. Thus the listener cannot construe their position as intentional.
(d) Bracketing movements $18^{b}$, $21^{b}$ with $23^{f}$, $25^{b}$ distorts the chiasmus. In the 'centrepiece'

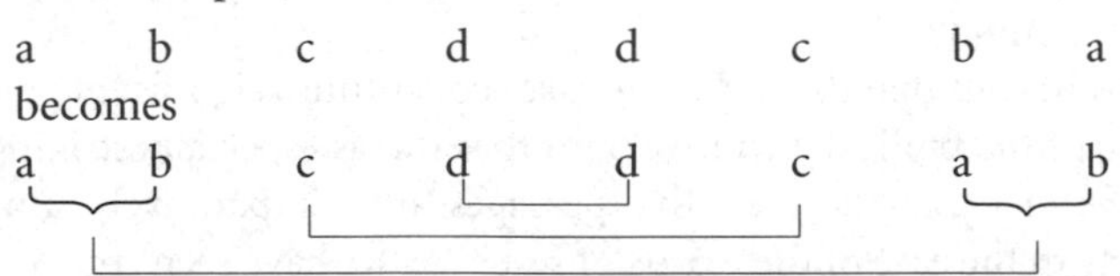


There is no evidence to suggest that Bach was prepared to consider a modified form of this kind as an allegory of the cross of Christ. Of course, it would be very easy to dispose of this difficulty if one simply construed the vocal thematic resemblance, and not the instrumental four-bar pattern, as the element that creates the symmetry. But how is an 'attentive listener' supposed to arrive at this conclusion?

On the other hand, Bach did not attempt to modify the veiled nature of the symmetrical relationship, nor for that matter to make it more obvious. If he had merely wished to emphasize the symmetry, then the transformation of movement $16^{d}$, 'Wir dürfen niemand töten', into an adjunct of movement $16^{b}$, 'Wäre dieser nicht ein Übeltäter', would have been a rather unfortunate decision, for it points the listener in the wrong direction (i.e. he is led to think that he is always required to perceive no more than two consecutive pairs of movements). Moreover, Bach could have taken movements $18^{b}$ and $23^{f}$ out of the framework of the four-bar model (see above under (d)). And then he could have created another pair of movements with $18^{b}$, 'Nicht diesen, sondern Barrabam', and $27^{b}$, 'Lasset uns den nicht zerteilen'. That he did nothing of the sort reinforces our doubts about whether he really attached as much importance to the symmetry of the turba choruses as we would sometimes like to think nowadays.

Furthermore, did Bach regard the symmetry of the 'centrepiece' as a musical form superimposed on the purposeful course of the action, or did he perceive it to be congruent with the biblical narrative? Smend believes in the second of these two possibilities, for he is of the opinion that the climax of the St John Passion is not only marked by the musical quality of the chorale 'Durch dein Gefängnis, Gottes Sohn', but also by a change of course in the action: prior to this Pilate attempts to release Jesus, and thereafter he gives way to the pressure of the crowd (see above, pp. 97–8). But this transforms the passion of Jesus of Nazareth into the tragedy of Pilate, who, torn between his duty (to release an innocent man) and his inclinations (to remain on good terms with the Emperor) makes a wrong decision. It is rather doubtful whether this is what Bach really had in mind.

Breig points out that the turba choruses constitute a significant part of the setting of the biblical narrative, and that this is especially striking in view of the fact that the recitative passages are comparatively simple, particularly in the case of the words of Jesus. As we have seen (pp. 62–4), these words (and those of Pilate) are far more strongly emphasized by composers such as Ritter and Mattheson. And finally, the scarcity of arias in the sections of the work to which the turba choruses are assigned underlines the significance of the latter.

All this leads us to the conclusion that the turba choruses of the St John Passion occupy an important position in the work and, on account of their numerous correspondences, are of significance with regard to its formal stability. It is less certain whether Bach, with the help of a partly natural (movements $21^{b}+25^{b}$, $21^{d}+23^{d}$) and partly consciously elaborated (movements $21^{f}+23^{b}$) symmetry, intended to impress on the whole work an axial symmetrical order that can be perceived by the listener; or whether he wished this order to be construed as a symbol of the cross of Christ. It is even less certain that Bach thus intended to shift the emphasis from the death of Jesus to Pilate's decision. In this regard Breig's interpretation seems to be far more convincing (1985: 88–91). He construes the order of the turba choruses as an image of St John's theological position, according to which Jesus arranged his return to the Father in a both systematic and prescient manner, so that his 'enemies, without knowing or wishing it, contribute to the realization of the divine plan of salvation'. Breig concludes: 'The symmetrical arrangement is a not unimportant feature of the correspondences between the turba choruses. However, to declare it to be the real or indeed the sole meaning of the correspondences amounts to adopting a constricted view of the matter.'

Moreover, one could also turn the question round the other way. Can the structure of the St John Passion in fact be deduced merely from the correspondence between the turba choruses, or do the other movements also have a function in the formal design?

I have already referred to Martin Petzoldt's remarks concerning the caesura-like function of certain chorales, which are posited on the idea that the passion narrative can be divided into five *actus*.[63] Of course, not all of the chorales have this function. Furthermore, the chorale 'In meines Herzens Grunde' (movement 26) comes unusually late as the end of the *actus* 'Pilatus', which is rather long in any case. Because it is heard three times, the chorale 'Jesu Leiden, Pein und Tod' occupies a pre-eminent position. Indeed, in Version II it is heard a fourth time, so that we are once again confronted with the makings of a symmetrical arrangement:

| 11$^{+}$. Aria + Chorale | 14. Chorale | 28. Chorale | 32. Aria + Chorale |
|---|---|---|---|
| Himmel reiße | | | Mein teurer Heiland |
| Jesu, deine Passion | Petrus, der . . . | Er nahm alles | Jesu, der du warest tot |

Yet it is doubtful whether Bach deliberately wished to add to the symmetry of the turba choruses in this way in 1725.

The disposition of the arias is rather striking. They are not distributed equally throughout the work, and always emphasize the decisive events of the passion narrative (see above, pp. 52–4). However, if we are prepared to interpret the disposition of the arias, the function of which is to provide moments of repose and an increasing awareness of the Passion narrative, as part of Bach's ground plan, we arrive at a design that, as it were, complements the order of the turba choruses. Whereas the inner sections of the Passion, including the majority of the turba choruses, seem to constitute a steadily progressing part of the narrative which, if at all, is held back only by the turba choruses themselves,[64] the framing sections are devoted to meditation. There is an unmistakable emphasis on the contemplation of the death of Jesus, so that the duplication of the ending in movements 39 and 40 seems to have been carefully premeditated.

I am thus of the opinion that the specific function of the arias, which Smend no more than hints at (though without emphasizing their 'complementary' order), is just as much part of the ground plan of the St John Passion as the function of the turba choruses, and this surely forces us to come to the conclusion that it is not the chorale 'Durch dein Gefängnis,

[63] In the case of movements 14 and 40 there can be no doubt about the fact that they function as endings.

[64] Was this perhaps the reason why Bach did not set the aria text 'Durch dein Gefängnis, Gottes Sohn' as an aria, but as a simple chorale?

Gottes Sohn' which is the climax of the work: it is the death of Christ, which is emphasized by three arias and an arioso.

That it is none the less possible to interpret the work as having been symmetrically planned, as Smend, Chafe, and others have done, does not, in my opinion, contradict what has just been said. As we have seen, great works of art can be interpreted in a number of different ways. Yet whether, over and above this, such symmetry—and especially the kind suggested by Chafe, which is based only on mechanical numbering and not on harmonic relationships—may be interpreted as a cruciform sign construed as such by Bach is probably one of the questions to which there will never be an answer.

At the end of this section of the chapter I return briefly to the problem of the compositional process in the St John Passion. Although it is impossible to give a categorical answer to the question of whether the work was 'planned in advance or composed in a sequence determined by the text', it would be true to say that we have now gained certain insights, and these enable us to come to certain conclusions.

First, the analysis of the work has produced nothing to suggest that there is room for doubt with regard to the supposition voiced above (p. 56), namely that Bach composed the Passion largely during the *tempus clausum* in Lent 1724. It is possible to state the following:

1. None of the texts written especially for the Passion and none of the settings in Version I necessarily point back to the time before 1724, and in particular to Bach's years in Cöthen.
2. There is no reason whatsoever to suppose that Bach composed a piece from the latter part of the work at an earlier stage, or that he put to one side a piece from the beginning to be composed later on.
3. The following is true of the turba choruses (if we disregard the need for overall planning):
   (a) The multiple use of the instrumental four-bar model does not in fact have to have been planned before its first repetition in movement $2^{d}$;
   (b) The creation of pairs of movements with identical vocal thematic material does not in fact have to have been planned before the final version of movement $16^{d}$ or (if earlier) before the composition of movement $23^{b}$;
   (c) The symmetry of the turba choruses is largely the result of the structure of the original biblical text, and Bach was not really in a position to change this.

Thus there is actually nothing to suggest that the work was not in fact composed on a movement-by-movement basis—and this means that the onus of proof rests on those who believe that the opposite is the case. However, this does not exclude the possibility that there was large-scale planning in certain areas. These include mapping out a tonal scheme for the whole work (even if I am unable to accept that the principles propounded by Chafe are those of Bach) and other considerations relating to the scoring, the sequence of movements, etc. (see also pp. 56–7). It is also obvious that, although the turba choruses (designed as pairs) were composed in sequence as the work progressed, the use of the second text was already taken into account in the original design.[65]

Compared with the composition of a corresponding number of cantatas, such planning naturally entailed some additional effort, though this still remained within limits which did not preclude a realization of the project in Lent 1724. If the hypothesis that the St Matthew Passion was composed over a period of more than two years (Chafe 1982) were quite unexpectedly to be confirmed,[66] it would prove that the genesis of this work was completely different from that of all previous vocal compositions by Bach, not only of the cantatas, but also, as we are now in a position to say, of the St John Passion.

## 5. PERFORMANCE PRACTICE

### *a. General Remarks*

The problems of performance practice in the St John Passion do not differ fundamentally from those of the cantatas[67] and Bach's other large choral works, though of course there is one striking difference. For the normal Sunday services the four choirs of St Thomas's School were assigned to four different churches, whereas a significantly larger number of singers was available for the performance of a Passion. However, we must bear in mind none the less that, apart from the first choir, only the second choir was in a position to tackle the difficult music of Bach's Passions. On the basis of what is now generally taken to have

[65] With the exception of movement 16$^{d}$, 'Wir dürfen niemand töten', which was only brought into line with movement 16$^{b}$ at a later stage.

[66] See esp. Chafe (1982: 105, 107, 111–12).

[67] See Alfred Dürr, *Die Kantaten von Johann Sebastian Bach* (Kassel and Munich, 1971; 6th edn., 1995), introduction, ch. 3.

been the case,[68] the number of singers would thus have been doubled from *c.*12 to *c.*24. However, these figures should not be taken literally, for Bach may well have assigned some of the instrumental parts to pupils from St Thomas's School, and this would have reduced the size of the choir. On the other hand, it is impossible to make out a case for a larger number of singers: the extant parts—two for each voice—would have proved insufficient for more than six singers in each voice category.

It is not quite clear how the singers of the figures who make only brief appearances in the work participated in the other movements. The part of the 'Ancilla' (movement 10) was sung by the solo soprano. Single parts have survived for 'Tenore Servus' (movement 10), and 'Basso Petrus & Pilatus'.[69] The fact that Bach writes either tacet or nothing at all for the singers of these parts in those movements in which they are not required does not of course mean that they sang only these minor roles and nothing else. Rather, it seems that Bach quite deliberately wanted to be able to decide from performance to performance—depending on the forces at his disposal and the abilities of the musicians concerned—where these singers could best be employed. The same is true of the musicians who played the viola d'amore, the viola da gamba, and the lute, and who also made only brief appearances. It cannot be excluded that the viola da gamba, with the exception of its solo in movement 30, participated throughout as a continuo instrument. If so, the musician must have played from one of the various continuo parts.

As far as we know, Bach first enlarged the normal instrumental forces on the occasion of the last performance, i.e. in Version IV (details in Ch. II. 3). By basing our calculations on the total number of extant parts and those that are presumably lost, we arrive at the figures shown on p. 109—which of course can only be approximate—with regard to Bach's smallest and largest instrumental forces (on the use of transverse flutes in Version I see also App. I).

[68] This has been called into question by Joshua Rifkin (see e.g., *Basler Jahrbuch für historische Musikpraxis* ix/1985 (Winterthur, 1986), 141–55), who maintains that a part was always designed for a single performer. Although this would seem to be corroborated by the minimum number of performers listed below, these are only approximate figures, for it cannot be excluded that some of the parts (esp. for the bc) are no longer extant. Moreover, Rifkin's hypothesis has not remained unchallenged.

[69] Both probably from Version IV, though they were no doubt designed to replace lost earlier parts.

Versions I to II:

| Voice/Instrument | No. of Parts (= Desks) | Approx. no. of performers |
|---|---|---|
| SATB soli | 1 each (=4) | 1–3 each (=4–12) |
| SATB in ripieno | 1 each (=4) | 1–3 each (=4–12) |
| T Servus | 1 | (1) |
| B Petrus & Pilatus | 1 | (1) |
| Fltr I, II | 1 each (=2) | 1 each (=2) |
| Ob (Ob d'am, Ob da c) I, II | 1 each (=2) | 1 each (=2) |
| Vn I, II | 2 each (=4) | 1–2 each (=2–4) |
| Va | 1 | 1–2 |
| Va d'am I, II | 1 each (=2) | (1 each =2) |
| Va da g | 1 | (1) |
| Liuto, later Org | 1 | (1) |
| Bc | 2 | 2–4 |
| Org | 1 | 1 |
| Version IV has the following variants: | | |
| Vn I | 3 | 3–6 |
| Va | 2 | 2–4 |
| 'Bassono grosso' | 1 | 1 |
| Cemb. | 1 | 1 |

Although performances with small orchestral forces of this kind are the exception nowadays, whereas those with a large number of performers (especially singers and strings) tend to be the rule, there is nothing to suggest that Bach, in his own performances, considered the forces at his disposal to be too small. In fact, when larger forces became available, he was more inclined to expand the musical structure than to strengthen the ripieno section.[70] Modern performers who favour large forces must take the consequences. The argument 'If Bach had had . . .' may be a common one, but it is totally impossible to prove.

Furthermore, there is the problematical question of whether or not the textual alterations in movements 9, 19, 20 (and 39?) correspond with Bach's intentions. In view of the illustrative quality of the music, the lack of congruity between the new texts and the existing composition makes it seem likely that Bach used them because he was forced to do so by the

[70] See esp. the St Matthew Passion, but also the passage in his submission to the Leipzig Town Council on 23 August 1730 in which he calls for three or, if possible, four singers per part 'so that if one happens to be ill . . . it will still be possible to sing a double-chorus motet' (*Dok.* i, no. 22, p. 60). This shows that Bach was quite prepared to accept the possibility of having only one singer per part.

authorities. For this reason musicians will tend to go back to the original texts, even though this means abandoning the principle of adhering to the composer's final version (*Fassung letzter Hand*). However, in the final analysis the assumption on which this decision is based remains a hypothetical one (see above, pp. 49–50).

### *b. The Execution of the Continuo*

The incomplete nature of the transmitted material and the fact that most of the extant parts are merely entitled 'Continuo' (one part, in addition to the one with the correct heading 'Cembalo', is also and obviously incorrectly entitled 'Cembalo') means that there is some room for conjecture.

It may be taken for granted that at least one cello and one violone were involved in the execution of the bc.[71] They will have been joined by an organ, whose part is no longer extant, though it can be reconstructed. A harpsichord may well have been used from the very beginning: Bach himself may have played it from the score in Versions I to III, though a separate part was copied out for Version IV (probably on account of Bach's failing eyesight).

It is also legitimate to assume that, from Version I onwards, there was at least one bassoon (see n. 71, above), and that the player used one of the continuo parts. Version IV calls for an (additional?) 'bassono grosso'. This was probably a double bassoon, though it may also have been a ripieno bassoon designed to complement a (normal) bassoon which (with some exceptions) played throughout the work (see also p. 9 n. 13).

These observations confirm the general impression that Bach favoured a relatively large continuo group, and this is diametrically opposed to the custom (which persists to this day) of accompanying all of the recitatives and almost all of the arias with nothing but a solo cello and harpsichord. Admittedly, modern instruments, especially the double bass and the bassoon, are considerably louder than their baroque predecessors. Nevertheless, in solo movements one should, if at all possible, include a discreet 16' reinforcement of the continuo.

With regard to the execution of the recitative accompaniment, as in Bach's other sacred works there is no convincing answer to the question of whether the accompanying chords (including the bass notes) should

[71] In score A (*c.*1739) Bach notes in movement 1 'Violoncelli e Bassoni' and 'Org e Violone', which, if taken literally, would signify that there were several violoncellos and bassoons, and only one (organ and) violone.

be held for their full length, whether they should only be struck briefly, or whether the bass notes ought perhaps to be held for their full length, and the chords struck briefly.[72] As the theorists, roughly speaking, tended to prescribe 'holding' the notes at the beginning of the eighteenth century (Johann David Heinichen, 1711) and 'lifting' them towards the end of the eighteenth century (Christoph Gottlieb Schröter, 1772), the possibility cannot be excluded that Bach changed his mind on the subject, possibly in 1735 (Ascension Oratorio) or in 1736 (St Matthew Passion).

It seems natural, especially in the light of Bach's practice in the St Matthew Passion (1736), to assume that there should be a degree of differentiation in the St John Passion, so that the notes are held in case of the words of Jesus, and struck briefly in all the other recitative passages. This is sometimes done in modern performances. I none the less hesitate to describe this solution as being closest to Bach's intentions in deference to the contrast between the recitatives and the turba choruses described above. Did Bach perhaps consciously renounce any attempt to emphasize the words of Jesus in order to maintain this contrast?

I thus consider it to be better to accompany the recitatives either as notated throughout (i.e. with held notes) or in abbreviated form throughout, possibly with full-length bass notes.[73]

*c. Specific Problems*

Movement 13: 'Ach, mein Sinn'

With regard to the scoring, score A states 'Aria tutti li Stromenti', a stipulation that the copyist no doubt took over from the original score X. However, in view of the fact that the extant woodwind parts produced for Version II contain a tacet mark, which of course initially applied to

[72] The best survey of current research (and bibliography) is provided by Emil Platen, 'Aufgehoben oder ausgehalten?', in Reinhold Brinkmann (ed.), *Bachforschung und Bachinterpretation heute: Bericht über das Bachfest-Symposium 1978 der Philipps-Universität Marburg* (Kassel, 1981), 167–77. As the theoretical evidence, which is rather plentiful (though fairly scarce in Bach's lifetime), makes it difficult to discuss the subject in a rational manner, the argument tends to be conducted largely on an emotional level and on the basis of sources selected to confirm the position one happens to have adopted.

[73] This solution, a compromise, is suggested by the performing material produced on the basis of the *NBA* (Bärenreiter, Kassel), though with the added proviso that—with the exception of the organ part (!?)—the long notated bass notes should be 'shortened—in keeping with modern [?] practice'. Here again the performers will have to come to some kind of decision, and emend the parts accordingly.

movement $13^{II}$, though it was not subsequently altered. Bach must have decided, at the latest when he came to Version IV, to have the movement played without flutes and oboes.[74] It might perhaps be possible to subscribe to the hypothesis that Version I originally called for woodwind instruments, and that in Version IV Bach merely forgot that the tacet marks for movement $13^{II}$ should have been replaced by a reference to the relevant instrument.[75] If this were true, the participation of woodwind instruments could not be faulted nowadays. On the other hand, if present-day conductors omit the woodwinds, there is no reason why they should be accused of disregarding the information supplied in the score, although they are criticized for doing so. They have the evidence of the original parts on their side.

The old-fashioned notation of the following figure ♫.♪, which occurs frequently, should, in keeping with contemporary practice, be played thus: 𝄾♫.♪

Movements 19, 20: 'Betrachte, meine Seel'—'Erwäge, wie sein blutgefärbter Rücken'

The use of viola d'amore I, II and (in movement 19) of the lute is stipulated in score A (their inclusion surely derives from the original score X) and is evidently valid for Version I, though the relevant parts are no longer extant. In Version II both movements were replaced by movement $19^{II}$, and from Version III onwards Bach exchanged the violas d'amore for muted violins, and the lute for the organ (Version III, and Version IV?) or the harpsichord (Version IV?). It seems appropriate to view the replacement of the original instruments as a makeshift solution to which the modern performer should adhere only if he finds himself confronted with the same problems as Bach. With regard to the continuo in movement 20, there is no hard-and-fast evidence pointing to the viola da gamba (the movement is not contained in the viola da gamba part), whereas a note, 'senza Violone', in one of the bc parts confirms the conjecture voiced above, namely that the participation of the violone in the other movements was deemed to be self-evident.

[74] No woodwind parts have survived for Version I. Versions II and III do not include this movement.

[75] The sources provide no information in this regard. Suggested scoring if woodwind instruments are to be included: fltr I, II and ob d'am I with vn I; ob d'am II with vn II. Bach probably never seriously entertained the idea of amplifying the scoring by including the violas d'amore and the lute. At the most he may have toyed with the idea of adding a viola da gamba to strengthen the continuo.

Movements 21$^{b}$, 25$^{b}$: 'Sei gegrüßet' and 'Schreibe nicht'

In Versions III and IV the woodwind parts were each strengthened by a desk (1 or 2 violins?) of violin I. The other players in violin I continued to double the soprano.[76] Modern performances, which usually have a sufficiently large number of string players, would do well to follow Bach's example.

Movement 27$^{b}$: 'Lasset uns den nicht zerteilen'

All the extant bc parts (including *bassono grosso* and harpsichord) have only the simpler (crotchet) reading. The semiquaver figures are transmitted only in score A and without any indication of the scoring. There is a reference to an insert (which is no longer extant) in Continuo$^{I}$. It may have been removed when the part was being prepared 'pro Bassono grosso'. For musical reasons it seems logical to assign the part to a cello, though other possibilities (bassoon? viola da gamba?) cannot be discounted. Only *bassono grosso* and harpsichord do not come into question, as is demonstrated by the relevant parts.

Movement 30: 'Es ist vollbracht'

Two different versions of the viola da gamba part of the middle section, 'Der Held aus Juda siegt mit Macht' (bb. 20–39), have been transmitted. Score A envisages the gamba taking the continuo part, surely in accordance with the original score X and the parts of Versions I and II, which are also no longer extant. Bach himself then wrote out a new part, probably for Version III, in which the viola da gamba doubles the alto part an octave lower. This is probably the reason why the older part was discarded and replaced by a new one.

The reason why Bach changed his mind remains a mystery, and as far as we know, no modern performances have adhered to his instructions in this regard. Doubling the alto part an octave lower is generally considered to produce unsatisfactory results. Despite all the possible objections, only two explanations can in fact be adduced.

Either Bach thought differently about it than we do—perhaps he was so concerned to emphasize the vocal part against the compact sonority of the strings (note the careful dynamic marks in the instrumental part) that he considered this to be a meaningful measure—or he intended the movement to be sung by a bass instead of an alto. If this were the case, then what he did would certainly be justified, even in terms of modern musical practice. However, there is nothing in the sources to suggest that

[76] Details of the somewhat unclear source findings in Mendel, *KB*, pp. 99–100.

Bach wanted to reassign the part thus. Indeed, the fact that it is immediately followed by movement 32, a bass aria, speaks against this hypothesis or calls for a supplementary one: should this movement be left out, or should it also be assigned to a different voice? As long as there is no hard-and-fast evidence we can at the most assume that Bach intended to reassign the movement to a different voice, but did not go ahead with the plan.

However, we can rule out the idea that Bach wished the bass clef of the viola da gamba part to be played an octave higher. If this had been the case, he could have continued to write the part in the alto clef. Notated only a tone higher than in the bass clef, this would have simplified matters for performer and scribe, especially in view of the fact that the original, the alto part, whichever one it may have been, must have been notated in the alto clef.

In the final analysis Bach's procedure remains an unsolved mystery.

Movement 35: 'Zerfließe, mein Herze'

The two obbligato parts were at various times assigned to different instruments:

Version I: Score A, doubtless following X, stipulates 'due Trav. | due Hautb. da Caccia'. Mendel in fact mentions the possibility of an original scoring that involved violas d'amore I and II (*KB*, p. 110—this would mean that the scoring indication in X was changed at a later date into the one transmitted by A). Similarly, Smend conjectured that Bach originally used an oboe instead of a flute (see below, p. 116). However, these are nothing more than hypothetical explanations designed to make the possibility of an original version without transverse flutes seem plausible.

Version II: In contrast to the indications in A, the two parts occur only in transverse flute I and oboe [da caccia] I. Thus it seems that Bach did not envisage the use of all four instruments simultaneously.

Version III: The aria was omitted together with the interpolation from St Matthew (movement 33).

Version IV: As in Version II, though the transverse flute was doubled by violin I 'col sourdino' (which was probably a solo part), presumably for reasons connected with the tonal balance (the weak transverse flute contrasted with the robust oboe da caccia).

The scoring is therefore a matter for the contemporary performer to decide.

APPENDICES

# Problematical Points

## APPENDIX I: THE PARTICIPATION OF TRANSVERSE FLUTES IN VERSION I

The question of whether Version I of the St John Passion required the participation of transverse flutes was first mooted by Arthur Mendel. There are in fact very good reasons for such a question, and they concern both the sources and the music.

With regard to the sources, that the surviving original parts of Version I do not include flute parts is hardly surprising in view of the fact that the first copies of this version are no longer extant. The participation of transverse flutes is vouched for in the case of Version II by the existence of separate parts. However, the original score A is remarkably reticent when it comes to mentioning transverse flutes. True, an original wrapper, which usually carried a list of instruments, is no longer extant. Yet the autograph heading does not mention flutes, nor does the list of instruments at the start of the opening movement, which is written on 10 staves (2 oboes, 2 violins, viola, voices, bc) provide for their participation.

In the case of movement 9, the aria 'Ich folge dir gleichfalls', there is no scoring indication whatsoever in A. And in the fully scored movements 1, 2[b], 3, and 5 Bach also fails to indicate the participation of transverse flutes in the score, as indeed he fails to do (in line with his usual practice) in the rest of the chorales. The same applies to the majority of the movements in the score written by *Hauptkopist* H. Transverse flutes are mentioned only in the following movements:

- 21[a] staves 1–2: '2 Hautb. e Travers.'
- 21[d] tenor staff: 'due Traversi in octava sopra'
- 23[f] staff 1: 'Trav.'
- 25[b] staves 1–2: 'H. et Trav. 1. | H. et Trav 2'
- 34 staves 1–2: '2 Trav:'
- 35 staff 1: 'due Trav.'
- 39 staff 1, bar 61: 'Senza Hautb: e Trav:'—bar 113: 'Senz. H. et Trav:'

However, since the copyist's part of the score was first added for Version IV, only the fact that flutes are not mentioned, and not their presence, constitutes evidence pertaining to Version I.

With regard to the music, transverse flutes are in fact superfluous in a strikingly large number of movements, in which they do no more than double existing parts (movements 1, $2^{b}$, $12^{b}$, $16^{b}$, $16^{d}$, $18^{b}$, $21^{b}$, $21^{d}$, $21^{f}$, $23^{b}$, $23^{d}$, $25^{b}$, $27^{b}$, 39, and in all the chorales of Version I). If Bach, one is prompted to ask, had planned to include transverse flutes from the very beginning, would he not have made more frequent use of them on an independent basis?

A particularly striking feature is the doubling of the tenor part an octave higher, which occurs in movements $16^{b}$, $21^{d}$, $21^{f}$, $23^{b}$, $23^{d}$ and $27^{b}$. Here Mendel, I (pp. 47–8) rightly suggests that this was a makeshift solution, and that Bach may have chosen to emphasize the tenor in this way because the soprano and alto were already being strengthened sufficiently by the two oboes.

But the movements that have an independent flute part also pose a number of problems. In movement 9 ('Ich folge dir gleichfalls') the obbligato instrument, as we have seen, is not indicated in the score. Its key does not suit the baroque transverse flute, and its low register is not characteristic of the instrument. However, it is impossible to say which instrument Bach had in mind when he composed the aria. The use of the oboe is virtually ruled out on account of the use of (two) oboes in the aria that almost directly precedes it, 'Von den Stricken meiner Sünden' (movement 7). A violin is a distinct possibility because, surprisingly, it does not occur as a solo instrument anywhere else in the Passion, though the restricted range—the lowest note is d', at least in the extant version—makes it seem unlikely. Finally, to assume the use of a recorder presupposes that the surviving part was subjected to thoroughgoing revision.

Movements 34–5 ('Mein Herz, indem die ganze Welt'–'Zerfließe, mein Herze'). Despite the fact that the use of transverse flutes is mentioned here in A, the key, when compared with movement 9, is even more awkward, and the range even lower. Mendel (see Mendel, I and *KB*, 110) hints at the possibility of an original scoring with viola d'amore I and II instead of flute and oboe da caccia. However, this solution is hypothetical. It proffers an explanation, but adduces no conclusive proof. Friedrich Smend, whose findings rarely coincide with those of Mendel, also believed that there had once been a version without transverse flute, and suggested that an oboe had originally taken the place of the flute. This would turn the aria into a counterpart of movement 7 ('Von den Stricken meiner Sünden') (*Bachfestbuch* (Nuremberg, 1973), 91). In the light of other cases (e.g. Christmas Oratorio, movement 15), Smend's hypothesis seems more probable than that of Mendel. However, whereas it provides an explanation for the strikingly low range (if played by transverse flute), it fails to account for the unfavourable key, for the fingering on the baroque transverse flute was largely the same as that of the baroque oboe.

Only movement $23^{f}$ ('Wir haben keinen König denn den Kaiser') poses no problems with regard to transverse flutes. On the other hand, a comparison with movement 2[d] shows that it is perfectly possible to assume that the score originally lacked flutes, if, that is, the figured part (with the exception of the final note) is transposed down an octave.

* * *

Of course, it is also possible to challenge the idea that there was a first version without transverse flutes. In this case it would be necessary to ask whether the flutes participated (a) only in individual movements or (b) throughout (i.e. in all the tutti passages and in the appropriate solo movements).

With regard to (a), there is no need to be surprised by the fact that Bach's heading does not list flutes if transverse flute players were not envisaged, and if two of the musicians merely played the transverse flute as and when required. After all, the violas d'amore, the lute, and the viola da gamba are not mentioned either, and presumably for the same reason. To be sure, this does not dispel the arguments relating to the unfavourable keys and the low register. Furthermore, it is impossible to find two musicians in the turba choral movement 23[f] who could have played the flute at this point because they were not needed elsewhere. Here we would have to fall back on the assertion (for which there is no proof whatsoever) that the original score X must have been emended at this point, and that Versions II (to IV) replaced Version I (without flutes). We would be forced to come to the same conclusion in the case of movement 33 (see App. II), though I am basically of the opinion that Part A, which was written by a copyist, reproduces Version I.

With regard to (b), under these circumstances (i.e. flutes participating in the tutti passages throughout) it would be rather difficult to account for their absence in heading A and their frequent *colla parte* employment. Thus the most obvious solution would be to assume that Bach did not in fact envisage the participation of flutes when he began to compose the work (and then, in A, copied the heading from X without thinking), perhaps because he was still unsure about whether or not he would have any flautists at his disposal. At the earliest from movement 9, more probably from movement 21[b], but at the latest from movement 23[f] onwards he then began to include transverse flutes. Even so, the unfavourable key and register in the solo movements continues to be inexplicable, especially in aria 35, which under these circumstances would have been intended for the transverse flute from the start.

In point of fact, the assumption that Bach changed his mind and decided to make use of transverse flutes as he composed the work, is less startling than it might seem at first sight. Thus, for example, Bach initially wrote Cantata no. 128, 'Auf Christi Himmelfahrt allein' (1725) without woodwind instruments; the oboes first made an appearance when the parts were copied out. And the classic instance of a work without flutes, to which two flute parts were added when the parts were written out, is Part II of the Christmas Oratorio. In the score, at any rate, the staff of the instrumental obbligato part in the aria 'Frohe Hirten, eilt, ach eilet' at first bore no scoring indication.[1]

However, the most striking parallel—because the date is very close to Good Friday, 1724—is Cantata no. 67, 'Halt im Gedächtnis Jesum Christ', which was written for Low Sunday (16 April 1724). Here again Bach first decided to include a transverse flute as the work progressed,[2] in fact, so it seems, when he began to compose movement 6, in which the flute is required to execute an independent part.[3] However, at a later stage—when the part was copied out—the transverse flute was also assigned to the opening movement. Here we come across a phenomenon that also occurs in the St John Passion: where the instruments double the voices *colla parte*, the transverse flute doubles the tenor at the octave, obviously because the soprano and the alto are already being reinforced by the oboes d'amore.

* * *

With regard to the question of the participation of transverse flutes in Version I, it must be borne in mind that, as far as we know, Bach had not employed transverse flute players in Leipzig prior to this (in contrast to his time in Cöthen). In fact, it seems that he did not have a single good flautist at his disposal when he took up his duties as cantor of St Thomas's. The transverse flute first occurs in April 1724, either in the St John Passion (7 April) or in Cantata no. 67 (16 April). In the second half of the year Bach then began to display a predilection for the instrument, and wrote some especially interesting obbligato parts.[4]

When we weigh up the arguments for and against Mendel's suggestion, we are forced to concede that the matter cannot be resolved. True, it seems rather implausible that Bach wanted to include transverse flutes on a permanent basis from the moment he began to compose the work (see in particular the heading in score A). But whether he in fact decided to include them as late as 1725, or, and this seems far more plausible, while he was writing out the original score X, remains an unanswered question.

On the other hand, the compromise solution alluded to above—that Bach instructed two musicians who normally played other instruments to switch to the transverse flute from time to time—seems less plausible, for it fails to explain the nature of movement 23[f]. In fact, it requires an additional hypothesis, namely that this movement was different in Version I, although at this stage the Passion in principle already envisaged the use of transverse flutes.

[1] See Crit. Reports, *NBA* I/10 and II/6.

[2] See Alfred Dürr, 'Zur Bach-Kantate "Halt im Gedächtnis Jesum Christ" BWV 67', *Musik und Kirche*, 53 (1983), 74–7.

[3] The heading of the autograph score does not mention instruments. However, the wrapper inscribed by Johann Andreas Kuhnau has the term 'Traversa' at the usual place.

[4] See Dürr (cited in n. 2, above) which also refers to further literature on the subject.

## APPENDIX II: THE RECONSTRUCTION OF MOVEMENT 33 IN VERSION I

Movement 33, one of the textual interpolations in St John's account of the Passion, tells of the veil of the temple being rent in twain. It was transmitted in the continuo part of Version I (Mendel, *KB*: part B 21) in a three-bar version. Subsequently, in Version II, as is revealed by the sources of 1725, the three-bar version in Continuo[I] was crossed out and replaced by a reference to an inserted sheet that is no longer extant, and which no doubt contained the seven-bar movement of Versions II and IV. Most of the other extant parts of Set I originally had three bars' rest for the duration of movement 33. Thus the idea that there was an accidental error in Continuo[I] is out of the question. The part of the Evangelist (and the tenor part that went with it) is no longer extant.

Mendel, *KB* (p. 270) comes to the following (and to my mind correct) conclusions. The familiar interpolation in Versions II and IV with the text from Matt 27: 51–2 would be too long, even if it were abbreviated and restricted to verse 51.[1] However, it is perfectly possible to fit the parallel text from Mark 15: 38 into the three bars, as Mendel, *KB* (p. 270) demonstrates:

This proves that in Version I the second interpolation in the text of St John's Gospel did not come from St Matthew, but from St Mark. But this, admittedly, leads to another problem. Movement 34, the arioso 'Mein Herz, indem die ganze Welt', refers to an even greater extent than in Version II or Version IV, with which we are familiar, to matters that have in fact never been mentioned prior to this. Compare the juxtapostion on p. 119.

[1] Unless we assume, though this is quite implausible, that the Evangelist had to complete the recitative during the demisemiquaver run.

| Movement 34 | Matt. 27 | Mark 15 | Luke 23 | John |
|---|---|---|---|---|
| Mein Herz, indem die ganze Welt | | | | |
| Bei Jesu Leiden gleichfalls leidet, | | | | |
| Die Sonne sich in Trauer kleidet, | 45 | 33 | 44–5[a] | — |
| Der Vorhang reißt, | 51 | 38 | 45[b] | — |
| der Fels zerfällt, | 52 | — | — | — |
| Die Erde bebt, | 52 | — | — | — |
| die Gräber spalten, | 52 | — | — | — |
| Weil sie den Schöpfer sehn erkalten, | | | | |
| Was willst du deines Ortes tun? | | | | |

Clearly, the text of movement 34 (and not 35!) was written with St Matthew's account in mind; in fact, to be precise, the whole of St Matthew's account, for verse 45 is still missing in the longer version of movement 33. The reason for this is that the arioso is modelled on Brockes (see above, p. 47), at least with regard to the eclipse of the sun and the rocks that were rent. The other events are not mentioned here either. However, that Bach did in fact value the congruence between biblical narrative and meditative poetry[2] is demonstrated by the alterations he made in Version III after the removal of the interpolations from St Matthew. The ensuing arias and the arioso had to be replaced. Indeed, not even the words of St John, 'und alsobald krähete der Hahn' ('and immediately the cock crew') sufficed, so it seems, in Bach's (or the censor's) opinion to allow an aria about St Peter's remorse to follow, once the phrase 'Da gedachte Petrus . . .' ('And Peter remembered . . .') had been excised.

In the light of these remarks we may safely assume that in movement 33 of Version II Bach himself replaced the text of Mark 15: 38 with that of Matt. 27: 51–2 and changed the composition in order to make the connection with the following arioso closer and more logical.

## APPENDIX III: THE CHRONOLOGY OF THE PASSIONS BACH PERFORMED IN LEIPZIG

It is not as yet possible to give a complete list of the Passions that Bach performed in the main Leipzig churches. The following dates have been ascertained so far (see *Dok.* ii, no. 180, pp. 140–1):

1724 (7.4): St John Passion, Version I (Dürr, *Chr*², 67)
1725 (30.3): St John Passion, Version II (Dürr, *Chr*², 79)
1726 (19.4): Keiser, St Mark Passion (Dürr, *Chr*², 86)
1727 (11.4): St Matthew Passion ? (Dürr, *Chr*², 95, N 22: J. Rifkin)

[2] The St John Passions by Ritter and Mattheson were different in this respect. See above, Ch. 3 n. 5.

1728 (26.3): St John Passion, Version III—or 1732? (Mendel, *KB*)
1729 (15.4): St Matthew Passion? (Dürr, *Chr*², 98)
1730 (7.4): Anonymous, St Luke Passion, BWV 246 (A. Glöckner, *BJ* (1981), 70)
1731 (23.3): St Mark Passion (Dürr, *Chr*², 101; printed text)
1732 (11.4): See above, 1728
1733 (3.4): No performance on account of state mourning
1734 (23.4): No information
1735 (8.4): Possibly Anonymous, St Luke Passion, BWV 246 (Dürr, *Chr*², 110)
1736 (29.3): St Matthew Passion (Crit. Report *NBA* II/5)
1737 (19.4): No information
1738 (4.4): No information
1739 (27.3): St John Passion planned? (Mendel, *KB*)
1740 (15.4): No information
1741 (31.3): No information
1742 (23.3): St Matthew Passion (Y. Kobayashi, *BJ* (1988), 50)
1743 (12.4): No information
1744 (27.3): No information
1745 (16.4): No information
1746 (8.4): No information
1747 (31.3): No information
1748 (12.4): Handel/Keiser, Pasticcio? (A. Glöckner, *BJ* (1977), 91)
1749 (4.3): St John Passion, Version IV (Y. Kobayashi, *BJ* (1988), 63)
1750 (27.3): No information

There was also a revival of the anonymous St Luke Passion, BWV 246, in the 1740s. Not included in this list are the performances of passion music (which, if they were in fact directed by Bach, did not take place in one of the main churches) based on Barthold Heinrich Brockes by George Frideric Handel (and by Georg Philipp Telemann), the pasticcio passion after Karl Heinrich Graun, 'Wer ist der, so von Edom kömmt', and possibly another passion oratorio by Karl Heinrich Graun.[1]

The numerous questions that arise from this survey can be dealt with here only briefly.

### 1. *The Lost Passions*

That Bach left five passions to posterity, as the Obituary states (*Dok.* iii, no. 666, p. 86) is hardly open to doubt.[2] Even if the authors of the Obituary mistook the

[1] See Andreas Glöckner, 'Johann Sebastian Bachs Aufführungen zeitgenössischer Passionsmusiken', *BJ* (1977), 75–119.

[2] Although there was some doubt about the number of cantatas (see William H. Scheide, *Mf* 14 (1961), 60–3), the authors must have been fully aware of how many Passions Bach had written.

St Luke Passion, BWV 246, for a genuine work by Bach,[3] two works still remain unaccounted for: the St Mark Passion, BWV 247, and an unknown one. In all probability, we must consider three such works as lost. In contrast to the cantatas, whose extant cycles come mainly from 1723–6, only one Passion was written at this time: the St John Passion. The lost passions (with the possible exception of a Weimar work) can be assigned at the earliest to 1728, though probably to the 1730s, and perhaps to an even later date. There is no reliable information on this point. However, they would no doubt help to fill in some of the gaps in the above list of performances.

## 2. *The Unvarying Succession of the Gospels*

The 'Catalogue of Passions' by Telemann cited by Hörner (in Ch. 3 n. 4, above) demonstrates that from 1722 to 1767 Hamburg adhered to an unvarying succession of settings of the four evangelists: Matthew, Mark, Luke, and John. The question thus arises whether it is possible to assume a similar pattern in the case of the main churches in Leipzig. If so, a custom of this kind, or perhaps its intended introduction, might explain certain occurrences, e.g. the performance of the St John Passion in two successive years (1724 and 1725), which might have been done in order to return to the prescribed rotation. Furthermore, the interpolations from St Matthew may have been eliminated in order to retain an 'unadulterated' Gospel text on account of a prospective performance of a St Matthew Passion the following year.

Unfortunately, the extant sources do not substantiate such a supposition. In fact, they do the opposite. For a start, the two successive performances of Kuhnau's St Mark Passion in 1721 and 1722, if Schering's information is correct,[4] could perhaps have been due to Kuhnau's illness and death. If, for the sake of the argument, a performance of a St Luke Passion had been envisaged for 1723, then a St John Passion would have been due in 1724, but not in 1725. Here again one could at the most resort to a makeshift explanation, i.e. that Bach's St Matthew Passion was planned for 1725 (for which there is not a single shred of evidence!) and was not finished in time. Under these circumstances it might be possible to justify the idea that a St Mark Passion (by Reinhard Keiser) was due in 1726. Although Joshua Rifkin is not of this opinion, a St Luke Passion would thus have been due in 1727. A St John Passion in 1728 and a St Matthew Passion in 1729 would still fit into such a scheme, but not a St Luke Passion in 1730 or a St Mark Passion in 1731. Furthermore, the handful of dates established for the following years (St Matthew Passion 1736, 1742) does not fit in with the proposed scheme either. In short, the proffered hypothesis is based on assumptions about so many

[3] This is quite implausible, for C. P. E. Bach, one of the authors of the Obituary, was also involved in making Bach's copy of the score.

[4] See Schering, *L*, p. 165. However, it is no longer possible to verify Schering's source, and thus it cannot be ruled out that he made a mistake.

exceptions that it seems difficult to give credence to it. For this reason we will not pursue the matter any further.

### 3. *Performances of Passions without Biblical Texts*

As the list of performances cited above demonstrates, passions without biblical texts—Telemann called them 'wholly poetic' (Hörner [cited in Ch. 3 n. 4, above], 57)—were performed in Hamburg only in addition to, and never in place of, passions given in church services that retained the text of the Gospels. The notion that the main Leipzig churches were more liberal in this respect must be regarded as highly unlikely until such time as documents to the contrary become available.

Of course, it cannot be ruled out that Bach, particularly after he had become director of the students' Collegium musicum in 1729, may have put on non-liturgical passion performances in addition to his ecclesiastical duties. However, there is no evidence of this. Andreas Glöckner (*BJ* (1977), 105 ff.) assigns a performance of Handel's Brockes Passion to '*c.*1746–7', though the evidence presented is not entirely conclusive. The facts are as follows (numbering of movements as in HHA 1/7): Aria no. 3 is sung twice, the first verse after movement 2, the second after movement 4. Bach's scoring indication in the score (SBB Mus. ms. 9002/10, p. 8) is slightly misleading: 'Aria | due Oboe | due Violini | e | Viola | e Soprano | Tenore'. After movement 4 Bach (p. 11) wrote 'repetatur Aria | la Strofa 2 | in Soprano'. Glöckner takes this to be a reference to a lost soprano part once in the possession of Bach, and deduces that a set of parts was copied out. This would in fact suggest that there had been a performance (conducted by Bach). However, the text of the second verse was subsequently entered in the score by Carl Philipp Emanuel Bach. Thus the evidence can be interpreted in a variety of ways:

(a) As suggested by Glöckner. However, this does not necessarily point to an unaltered performance of the whole Passion (admittedly, the aria is not contained in the pasticcio based on Keiser and Handel).
(b) As a reference to a soprano part in the material from which the parts were copied. The text was to be taken from this source.
(c) As a reference to the scoring of the aria. Thus the first verse would have been sung by a tenor, and the second by a soprano (cf. the annotation at the beginning of the aria).

In short, Glöckner may very well be right. However, the passage he cites is too isolated and ambiguous to constitute sufficient and compelling proof for the rather far-reaching claim that, in addition to performances of passions in church, Bach directed passion performances that were 'not part of his normal schedule'. Indeed, the fact that Bach performed a pasticcio consisting of seven arias from Handel's Brockes Passion and a large part of Reinhard Keiser's St Mark Passion (Glöckner *BJ* (1977), 91 and 109–13) actually seems to suggest that the opposite was true, or, to put it rather more guardedly, that he had need of passions that employed the biblical text. The relevant document, a harpsichord part written by Johann Christoph Friedrich Bach (1732–95), points to the late 1740s, especially on account of the scribe's age. Therefore it is fairly certain either that the Leipzig authorities insisted on retaining the literal text of the Gospel at evensong on Good Friday in the principal churches until the end of Bach's life, or that Bach himself wanted to retain it.

In this context we should briefly examine the question (which continues to be a controversial issue) of whether Bach set to music a passion by Christian Friedrich Henrici in the style of Brockes, 'Erbauliche Gedancken Auf den Grünen Donnerstag und Charfreytag Uber den Leidenden JESUM, in einem ORATORIO Entworffen Von Picandern, 1725'.[5] It is fairly certain that he did not, and for the following reasons:

1. Bach could not have used it at evensong on Good Friday because other passions were performed in 1724, 1725, and 1726.
2. Until he assumed responsibility for the Collegium musicum early in 1729, Bach did not have the slightest reason to perform passions other than the ones heard at evensong on Good Friday. The time he had to devote to the composition of music for church services would hardly have permitted him to do so.
3. After Picander's text for the St Matthew Passion appeared, which was in 1729 at the latest, Bach was probably no longer interested in the 1725 text.

Thus I am of the opinion that, until a document to the contrary appears, we must reject the notion that 'Erbauliche Gedancken' (1725) was set to music by Bach.

## APPENDIX IV. THE PROBLEM OF SYMMETRY IN BACH'S WORK

There are various kinds of mathematical symmetry. However, in this context we are concerned only with axial symmetry. This signifies that every point on one side of an imaginary central axis corresponds to a similar one on the other side, at the same distance and on the same level.

Unearthing symmetrical forms and tonal patterns in early music, especially in that of Bach and Handel, has become a favourite twentieth-century pastime. It was originally a result of the anti-Romantic tendencies of the first half of the century, which rejected emotional enjoyment as inappropriate to pre-Romantic music. The listener was supposed to concentrate on the musical structures. This, it was thought, would enable him to understand both the composer's creative process, and the expectations of the eighteenth-century audience.

Formal symmetry has repeatedly been described as being of especial

[5] Repr. in Spitta, ii. 873–81 [not in Eng. trans.].

significance for Bach's music.[1] One of the main reasons for this is the fact that it is perceived to be a symbol of the Christian faith. Werner Breig has remarked (1985: 65, footnotes omitted):

> The word 'symmetrical' that Smend used in his study of the *St John Passion* [Smend 1926] was replaced from the time of his study of the *St Matthew Passion* (1928) onwards with the term '*chiastic-cyclic*' that had originally been introduced by Spitta. And in his discussion of the *Symbolum Nicenum* in the B minor Mass (1937) he construed the chiastic form as the framework of the *Crucifixus* movement and thus as a direct allusion to the cross of Christ. This prepared Smend for the final interpretative step, which he undertook in 1947 in his essay 'Luther and Bach'. The chiastic shape is now always construed as a symbol of the name and the cross of Christ, first on account of the phonetic significance of the letter X (Chi), which is the initial letter of the name of Christ, and secondly on account of its cruciform shape.

Reference also tends to be made to undeniable parallels in architecture, especially to the shape of baroque palaces such as Versailles, which suggest that formal symmetry, over and above its musical uses, was a pattern that was fundamental to the baroque aesthetic.

The classic examples in Bach have often been discussed and are well known. They range from the general form of the da capo aria via the Actus Tragicus (BWV 106) and the motet 'Jesu, meine Freude' (BWV 227) to the Credo of the B minor Mass (BWV 232$^{II}$) and beyond. For example, Walter Blankenburg portrays all the six parts of the Christmas Oratorio as symmetrical forms, and in addition parts I–III taken as a whole.[2] And finally, last but not least, there is the St John Passion, whose formal structure is the reason for this digression.

In addition to specific doubts about the notion that the perceived formal symmetry in the St John Passion corresponds to Bach's intentions (this has been discussed above), the critical reader will be prompted to ask whether scholars have not in fact accorded undue importance to this particular phenomenon, although it was no doubt of great importance for Bach!

The frequent comparison between a baroque palace and a da capo aria demonstrates that there are inescapable differences between architecture and music. A baroque palace presents its symmetry to us immediately, whereas the details are perceived at a later stage. However, a da capo aria can be defined as such in formal terms only when the last note has died away. Prior to this the listener has to piece together the details that are initially perceived individually. The palace is entered by a central doorway, and the wings are its adjuncts. The da capo aria, on the other hand, is 'entered' via the 'wings' (as if the listener were

[1] The studies by Friedrich Smend in *BJ* (1926) (BWV 245), (1928) (BWV 244), (1933) (BWV 769a), (1937) (BWV 232), and Smend (1947) are typical examples of this. See also numerous publications by Walter Blankenburg, esp. 'Die Symmetrieform in Bachs Werken und ihre Bedeutung', *BJ* (1949/50), 24–39; repr. in id., *Kirche und Musik* (Göttingen 1979), 183–97).

[2] Walter Blankenburg, *Das Weihnachts-Oratorium von Johann Sebastian Bach* (Kassel and Munich, 1982); see the formal patterns on pp. 39 (Parts I–III), 41 (I), 55 (II), 77 (III), 95 (IV), 111 (V), 129 (VI).

a servant). However, this wing happens to be the main section (A). This is where the theme is introduced and the key defined. On the other hand, the central section (B) with its unstable thematic material and its modulating harmonies proves to be a 'corridor' that leads back to the stability of section A, which is repeated.[3]

In this context we cannot discuss the question of whether the unfolding of music in time in fact calls for a 'foreshortened perspective', or for the compression of the second half of a piece. In other words, could an 'abbreviated da capo' be construed as a feature that produces true formal symmetry?

The net result of all this is as follows. Formal symmetry certainly plays an important role in Bach. And it may well be that it should sometimes be understood as chiastic, that is, as an image of the letter X and thus as a symbol of Christ and of the Cross. Bach himself never referred to this subject, and thus arguments for (and if so, to what extent) or against it are merely hypothetical.

On the other hand, it seems misguided to treat Bach's symmetrical forms as if they were the most important feature of the music, in the light of which all the other formal categories fade into insignificance. Furthermore, symmetrical form occurs only in a small minority of cases. The vast majority of church cantatas begin with the most substantial movement. None of the following movements, right up to the simple final chorale, is its equal. On the other hand, the common pair of movements entitled 'Prelude and Fugue' is designed in terms of a final climax, and this is already suggested by the term 'prelude'.[4]

Finally, a note on the architectural significance of the key scheme. It is not particularly difficult to demonstrate that Bach's choice of keys is part of a meaningful order, and that this also displays aspects of symmetry, above all the return to the opening key at the very end. However, tonal and formal structure do not necessarily coincide. This is demonstrated by the fact that the identical tonality of the outer movements predominates in works which are actually based on arch forms. That formal and tonal symmetry do not have to coincide, even in cycles arranged on symmetrical principles, can be seen in the case of the Actus Tragicus. B♭ minor, the key that is farthest away from the tonic E♭ (choir pitch in both cases), first makes an appearance in the movement after the one which constitutes the centre in formal terms:

[3] See also 'Die symmetrische Gestaltung von Teil I bis III' in Blankenburg, ibid. 38–9. Can 'the abasement of God' (movement 17) really be compared to a dome, and the choruses 'Jauchzet, frohlocket' and 'Herrscher des Himmels' (movements 1 and 24) to nothing more than the wings of a palace?

[4] Even in the late works in which Bach is clearly making a conscious effort to improve the status of the prelude, he achieves no more than a balanced (though still heterogeneous) group of two pieces which are not arranged around a central axis.

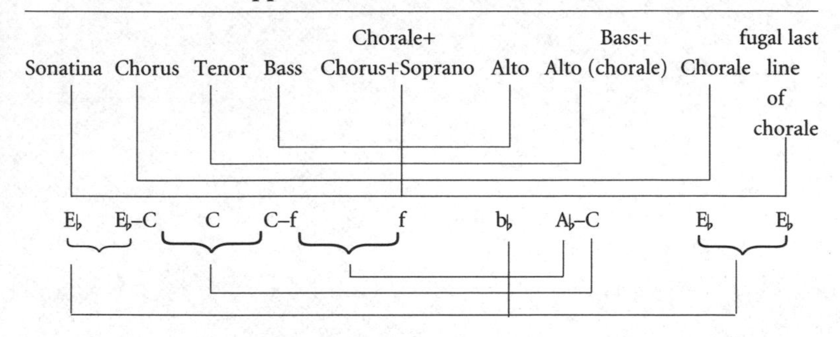


It is not surprising that there are similar differences in the case of the key scheme of the St John Passion, and thus it is clearly wrong to maintain that tonal symmetry is also revealed in Smend's 'centrepiece' (movements 16[e] to 27[e]; in Moser, 18[a] to 27[a]), for it flies in the face of all of the evidence.

# BIBLIOGRAPHY

*1. Editions*

In view of the variants it includes and the numbering of the movements, this book should be read in conjunction with the St John Passion as published in the *NBA*. See Abbreviations (*NBA*; Mendel, *KB*). Other editions, miniature scores, and vocal scores include those issued by the following publishers:

C. F. Peters, Leipzig (Hermann Kretzschmar),
Wiener Philharmonischer Verlag (Hermann Roth, 1924),
Eulenburg, Leipzig (Arnold Schering, 1925),
Schirmer, New York (Arthur Mendel, 1951),
Breitkopf & Härtel, Wiesbaden (Gerd Sievers, 1957).

*2. Literature*

The literature consulted when writing this book is referred to in the text and the footnotes. The following bibliography, which includes the works cited above, is a selection of suggestions for further reading. In addition to the specialized studies listed here, the reader is referred to the standard biographies by Philipp Spitta, Albert Schweitzer, Rudolf Steglich, Karl Geiringer, Alberto Basso, and others, though it must be remembered that those published before 1957 are still based on the old chronology. The same applies to certain articles and books in the present bibliography (and also to some written after 1957). The text of the St John Passion with appended critical apparatus is given in Werner Neumann (ed.), *Sämtliche von Johann Sebastian Bach vertonte Texte* (Leipzig, 1974), 236–44. Further literature on the subject of the Passion is listed in Christoph Wolff (ed.), *Bach-Bibliographie: Nachdruck der Verzeichnisse des Schrifttums über Johann Sebastian Bach (BJ 1905–1984). Mit einem Supplement und Register* (Berlin, 1985), in the bibliography on BWV 245 in the BWV, and in Hans-Joachim Schulze and Christoph Wolff, *Bach Compendium: Analytisch-bibliographisches Repertorium der Werke Johann Sebastian Bachs (BC): Vokalwerke*, pt. III (Leipzig, 1988).

*a. Literature on the theology of the passion as related by St John (Suggested reading)*

Becker, Jürgen, *Das Evangelium des Johannes: Ökumenischer Taschenbuch-Kommentar zum Neuen Testament 4/1 und 4/2* (Gütersloh, 1979, 1984)
Bultmann, Rudolf, *Das Evangelium des Johannes* (Göttingen, 1941; 1985[20])

Bultmann, Rudolf, *Theologie des Neuen Testaments* (Tübingen, 1953; 1984[9])
——'Johannesevangelium', *Die Religion in Geschichte und Gegenwart*, iii (Tübingen, 1959).
Schnackenburg, Rudolf, *Das Johannesevangelium*, vols. i–iii (Freiburg, 1979 ff.; numerous repr.).
Schulz, Siegfried, *Das Evangelium nach Johannes: Das Neue Testament Deutsch*, pt. 4 (Göttingen, 1983[15]).

*b. Literature on Bach scholarship and on the St John Passion*

Axmacher, Elke, *'Aus Liebe will mein Heyland sterben': Untersuchungen zum Wandel des Passionsverständnisses im frühen 18. Jahrhundert* (Beiträge zur theologischen Bachforschung, 2; Neuhausen and Stuttgart, 1984).
Blume, Friedrich, 'J. S. Bachs Passionen', in id., *Syntagma musicologicum, ii. Gesammelte Schriften und Reden 1962–1972*, ed. Anna Amalia Abert and Martin Ruhnke (Kassel, 1973).
Breig, Werner, 'Bemerkungen zur zyklischen Symmetrie in Bachs Leipziger Kirchenmusik', *Musik und Kirche*, 53 (1983), 173–9.
——'Zu den Turba-Chören von Bachs Johannes-Passion', *Geistliche Musik: Studien zu ihrer Geschichte und Funktion im 18. und 19. Jahrhundert, Hamburger Jahrbuch für Musikwissenschaft*, 8 (Laaber, 1985), 65–96.
Chafe, Eric, 'Key Structure and Tonal Allegory in the Passions of J. S. Bach: An Introduction', *Current Musicology*, 31 (1981), 39–54.
——'J. S. Bach's St. Matthew Passion: Aspects of Planning, Structure, and Chronology', *Journal of the American Musicological Society*, 35 (1982), 49–114.
——'Bach's St. John Passion: Theology and Musical Structure', in Don O. Franklin (ed.), *New Bach Studies* (Cambridge, 1988).
Darmstadt, Gerhart, 'Zur Aufführungspraxis der Johannes-Passion Johann Sebastian Bachs', *Musik und Kirche*, 53 (1983), 202–8.
Dibelius, Martin, 'Individualismus und Gemeindebewußtsein in Joh. Seb. Bachs Passionen', *Archiv für Reformationsgeschichte*, 41 (1948), 132–54; repr. in id., *Botschaft und Geschichte*, i (Tübingen, 1953).
Dürr, Alfred, *Zur Chronologie der Vokalwerke J. S. Bachs*, 2nd edn., repr. of *BJ* 1957 edn. with notes and addenda (Kassel, 1976).
Engelhardt, Walter, 'Das Arioso "Betrachte, meine Seel" der Bachschen Johannes-Passion (Nr. 31)', *Musik und Kirche*, 27 (1957), 136.
Fischer, Kurt von, 'Bachs Passionen im Lichte musikalischer und frömmigkeitsgeschichtlicher Traditionen', in id., *Johann Sebastian Bach: Welt, Umwelt und Frömmigkeit* (Jahresgabe 1982 der Internationalen Bach-Gesellschaft Schaffhausen; Wiesbaden, 1983), 13–23.
Fischer, Wilfried, 'Einführung in die Johannes-Passion von Johann Sebastian Bach', *Musik und Bildung*, 12/71 (1980), 225–9.
Frederichs, Henning, *Das Verhältnis von Text und Musik in den Brockes-Passionen Keisers, Händels, Telemanns und Matthesons* (Musikwissenschaft-

liche Schriften, 9; Munich and Salzburg, 1975).

Ganzhorn-Burkhardt, Renate, 'Zur Bedeutung der Choräle in Bachs Johannes-passion', *Musik und Kirche*, 53 (1983), 64–73.

Goldschmidt, Harry, 'Johannes-Passion: "Es ist vollbracht"—Zu Bachs obligatem Begleitverfahren', *Bericht über die Wissenschaftliche Konferenz zum III. Internationalen Bach-Fest der DDR, Leipzig 18./19. September 1975* (Leipzig, 1977), 181–8.

Melchert, Hermann, *Das Rezitativ der Bachschen Johannespassion* (Wilhelmshaven, 1988).

Mendel, Arthur, 'Traces of the Pre-History of Bach's St. John and St. Matthew Passions', in *Festschrift Otto Erich Deutsch zum 80. Geburtstag* (Kassel, 1963), 31–48.

—— 'More on the Weimar Origin of Bach's *O Mensch, bewein* (BWV 244/35)', *Journal of the American Musicological Society*, 17 (1964), 203–6.

—— 'Wasserzeichen in den Originalstimmen der Johannes-Passion Johann Sebastian Bachs', *Die Musikforschung*, 19 (1966), 291–4.

Meyer, Ulrich, *J. S. Bachs Musik als theonome Kunst* (Wiesbaden, 1979).

Moser, Hans Joachim, 'Zum Bau von Bachs Johannespassion', *BJ* (1932), 155–7.

Prinz, Ulrich, 'Zur Bezeichnung "Bassono" und "Fagotto" bei J. S. Bach', *BJ* (1981), 107–22.

Richter, Bernhard Friedrich, 'Zur Geschichte der Passionsaufführungen in Leipzig', *BJ* (1911), 50–9.

Schering, Arnold, *Johann Sebastian Bachs Leipziger Kirchenmusik: Studien und Wege zu ihrer Erkenntnis* (Leipzig, 1936).

—— *Johann Sebastian Bach und das Musikleben Leipzigs im 18. Jahrhundert* (Musikgeschichte Leipzigs, 3, Leipzig, 1941)

Schulze, Hans Joachim, 'Zur Aufführungsgeschichte von Bachs Johannes-Passion', *BJ* (1983), 118–19.

—— *Studien zur Bach-Überlieferung im 18. Jahrhundert* (Leipzig, 1984).

Smend, Friedrich, 'Die Johannes-Passion von Bach: Auf ihren Bau untersucht', *BJ* (1926), 105–28; repr. in id., *Bach-Studien: Gesammelte Reden und Aufsätze*, ed. Christoph Wolff (Kassel, 1969), 11–23.

—— 'Luther und Bach', *Der Anfang*, 2 (Berlin, 1947); repr. in Friedrich Smend, *Bach-Studien*, 153–75.

—— *Bach in Köthen* (Berlin, 1951) [Eng. trans. 1985].

—— 'Zur Passion nach dem Evangelisten Johannes', *Bachfestbuch* (Nuremberg, 1973), 89–92.

Stiller, Günther, *Johann Sebastian Bach und das Leipziger gottesdienstliche Leben seiner Zeit* (Kassel, etc., 1970)

Weiss, Dieter, 'Zur Tonartengliederung in J. S. Bachs Johannes-Passion', *Musik und Kirche*, 40 (1970), 33.

*Photographic Acknowledgements*

Staatsbibliothek zu Berlin—Preußischer Kulturbesitz, Music Division, Mus. ms. Bach P 28: p. 16
Staatsbibliothek zu Berlin—Preußischer Kulturbesitz, Music Division, Mus. ms. Bach St 111: pp. 22, 23, and 28.

JOHANN SEBASTIAN BACH

# Passio secundum Johannem

Die Satzzählung folgt *NBA*, dahinter in Klammern: Zählung des BWV (I. Auflage), zugleich der meisten älteren Druckausgaben.

Parte prima

1 (1). CHORUS [S, A, T, B; Fltr + Ob I; Fltr + Ob II; Str, Bc] g

Herr, unser Herrscher, dessen Ruhm
In allen Landen herrlich ist!
Zeig uns durch deine Passion,
Daß du, der wahre Gottessohn,
Zu aller Zeit,
Auch in der größten Niedrigkeit,
Verherrlicht worden bist!

2[a] (2). [RECITATIVO. T, B, Bc] c–g

Evangelista
*Jesus ging mit seinen Jüngern über den Bach Kidron, da war ein Garte, darein ging Jesus und seine Jünger. Judas aber, der ihn verriet, wußte den Ort auch, denn Jesus versammlete sich oft daselbst mit seinen Jüngern. Da nun Judas zu sich hatte genommen die Schar und der Hohenpriester und Pharisäer Diener, kommt er dahin mit Fackeln, Lampen und mit Waffen. Als nun Jesus wußte alles, was ihm begegnen sollte, ging er hinaus und sprach zu ihnen:*
Jesus
*Wen suchet ihr?*
Evangelista
*Sie antworteten ihm:*

JOHANN SEBASTIAN BACH

# St John Passion

The numbering of the movements is based on *NBA*. The numbering of the BWV (1st edn.), which is also that of most of the older printed editions, is given in parentheses.

Parte prima

1 (1). CHORUS [S, A, T, B; fltr + ob I; fltr + ob II; str, bc] G min C

O Lord our Governor, whose renown
Is excellent in all the earth!
Shew us through thy Passion,
That thou, the very Son of God,
In every age,
Even in the greatest lowliness,
Wast glorified!

2[a] (2). [RECITATIVO. T, B, bc] C min–G min C

Evangelista
*Jesus went forth with his disciples over the brook Cedron, where was a garden, into the which he entered, and his disciples. And Judas also, which betrayed him, knew the place: for Jesus oft-times resorted thither with his disciples. Judas then, having received a band of men and officers from the chief priests and Pharisees, cometh thither with lanterns and torches and weapons. Jesus therefore, knowing all things that should come upon him, went forth, and said unto them,*
Jesus
*Whom seek ye?*
Evangelista
*They answered him,*

2b (3). CHORUS [S, A, T, B, Ob I, II; Str + Fltr I + II; Bc] g

*Jesum von Nazareth.*

2c (4). [RECITATIVO. T, B, Bc] g–c

Evangelista
*Jesus spricht zu ihnen:*
Jesus
*Ich bins.*
Evangelista
*Judas aber, der ihn verriet, stund auch bei ihnen. Als nun Jesus zu ihnen sprach: Ich bins, wichen sie zurücke und fielen zu Boden. Da fregete er sie abermal:*

Jesus
*Wen suchet ihr?*
Evangelista
*Sie aber sprachen:*

2d (5). CHORUS [S, A, T, B, Ob I, II, Str, Bc] c

*Jesum von Nazareth.*

2e (6). [RECITATIVO. T, B, Bc] c–B

Evangelista
*Jesus antwortete:*
Jesus
*Ich habs euch gesagt, daß ichs sei, suchet ihr denn mich, so lasset diese gehen!*

3 (7). CHORAL [S, A, T, B, Bc (+ Instr)] g

**O große Lieb, o Lieb ohn alle Maße,**
**Die dich gebracht auf diese Marterstraße!**
**Ich lebte mit der Welt in Lust und Freuden,**
**Und du mußt leiden.**

4 (8). [RECITATIVO. T, B, Bc] B–d

Evangelista
*Auf daß das Wort erfüllet würde, welches er sagte: Ich*

2^b (3). CHORUS [S, A, T, B, ob I, II; str + fltr I + II; bc] G min C

*Jesus of Nazareth.*

2^c (4). [RECITATIVO. T, B, bc] G min–C min C

Evangelista
*Jesus saith unto them,*
Jesus
*I am he.*
Evangelista
*And Judas also, which betrayed him, stood with them. As soon then as he had said unto them, I am he, they went backward, and fell to the ground. Then asked he them again,*
Jesus
*Whom seek ye?*
Evangelista
*And they said,*

2^d (5). CHORUS [S, A, T, B, ob I, II, str, bc] C min C

*Jesus of Nazareth.*

2^e (6). [RECITATIVO, T, B, bc] C min–B♭ maj C

Evangelista
*Jesus answered,*
Jesus
*I have told you that I am he: if therefore ye seek me, let these go their way:*

3 (7). Chorale [S, A, T, B, bc (+ instr)] G min C

**O greatest love, o love that's never-ending,**
**Which thee hath brought unto this martyr's path!**
**I lived with the world in gladness and delight,**
**And thou must suffer.**

4 (8). [RECITATIVO, T, B, bc] B♭ maj–D min C

Evangelista
*That the saying might be fulfilled, which he spake, Of*

*habe der keine verloren, die du mir gegeben hast. Da hatte Simon Petrus ein Schwert und zog es aus und schlug nach des Hohenpriesters Knecht und hieb ihm sein recht Ohr ab; und der Knecht hieß Malchus. Da sprach Jesus zu Petro:*
Jesus
*Stecke dein Schwert in die Scheide! Soll ich den Kelch nicht trinken, den mir mein Vater gegeben hat?*

5 (9). CHORAL [S, A, T, B, Bc (+ Instr)] d

**Dein Will gescheh, Herr Gott, zugleich**
**Auf Erden wie im Himmelreich.**
**Gib uns Geduld in Leidenszeit,**
**Gehorsam sein in Lieb und Leid;**
**Wehr und steur allem Fleisch und Blut,**
**Das wider deinen Willen tut!**

6 (10). [RECITATIVO. T, Bc] F–d

Evangelista
*Die Schar aber und der Oberhauptmann und die Diener der Jüden nahmen Jesum und bunden ihn und führeten ihn aufs erste zu Hannas, der war Kaiphas Schwäher, welcher des Jahres Hoherpriester war. Es war aber Kaiphas, der den Juden riet, es wäre gut, daß ein Mensch würde umbracht für das Volk.*

7 (11). ARIA [A, Ob I, II, Bc] d

Von den Stricken meiner Sünden
Mich zu entbinden,
Wird mein Heil gebunden.
    Mich von allen Lasterbeulen
    Völlig zu heilen,
    Läßt er sich verwunden.

8 (12). [RECITATIVO. T, Bc] B–B

Evangelista
*Simon Petrus aber folgete Jesu nach und ein ander Jünger.*

*them which thou gavest me have I lost none. Then Simon Peter having a sword drew it, and smote the high priest's servant, and cut off his right ear. The servant's name was Malchus. Then said Jesus unto Peter,*

Jesus

*Put up thy sword into the sheath: the cup which my Father hath given me, shall I not drink it?*

5 (9). CHORALE [S, A, T, B, bc (+ instr)] D min C

**Thy will be done, Lord God, at once**
**On earth and in the heavens' realm.**
**Grant us patience in adverse times,**
**Obedience in love and pain;**
**Defend and keep all flesh and blood,**
**Which doth transgress against thy will.**

6 (10). [RECITATIVO. T, bc] F maj–D min C

Evangelista

*Then the band and the captain and officers of the Jews took Jesus, and bound him. And led him away to Annas first; for he was father in law to Caiaphas, which was the high priest that same year. Now Caiaphas was he, which gave counsel to the Jews, that it was expedient that one man should die for the people.*

7 (11). ARIA [A, ob I, II, bc] D min 3/4

From the bonds of my sins
To unbind me,
My Saviour is being bound.
From all the running sores of vice
Fully to heal me,
He allows himself to be wounded.

8 (12). [RECITATIVO. T, bc] B♭ maj–B♭ maj C

Evangelista

*And Simon Peter followed Jesus, and so did another disciple:*

9 (13). Aria [S; Fltr I + II; Bc] B

Ich folge dir gleichfalls mit freudigen Schritten
Und lasse dich nicht,
Mein Leben, mein Licht.
Befördre den Lauf
Und höre nicht auf,
Selbst an mir zu ziehen, zu schieben, zu bitten!

10 (14). [Recitativo. S, T, T, B, B, Bc] g–E

Evangelista
*Derselbige Jünger war dem Hohenpriester bekannt und ging mit Jesu hinein in des Hohenpriesters Palast. Petrus aber stund draußen für der Tür. Da ging der andere Jünger, der dem Hohenpriester bekannt war, hinaus und redete mit der Türhüterin und führete Petrum hinein. Da sprach die Magd, die Türhüterin, zu Petro:*
Ancilla
*Bist du nicht dieses Menschen Jünger einer?*
Evangelista
*Er sprach:*
Petrus
*Ich bins nicht.*
Evangelista
*Es stunden aber die Knechte und Diener und hatten ein Kohlfeu'r gemacht (denn es war kalt) und wärmeten sich. Petrus aber stund bei ihnen und wärmete sich. Aber der Hohepriester fragte Jesum um seine Jünger und um seine Lehre. Jesus antwortete ihm:*
Jesus
*Ich habe frei, öffentlich geredet für der Welt. Ich habe allezeit gelehret in der Schule und in dem Tempel, da alle Juden zusammenkommen, und habe nichts im Verborgnen geredt. Was fragest du mich darum? Frage die darum, die gehöret haben, was ich zu ihnen geredet habe! Siehe, dieselbigen wissen, was ich gesagt habe.*
Evangelista
*Als er aber solches redete, gab der Diener einer, die dabeistunden, Jesu einen Backenstreich und sprach:*

9 (13). Aria [S; fltr I + II; bc] B♭maj 3/8

I follow thee also with steps that are joyful,
And will not leave thee,
My life, my light.
Assist thou the path
And yet do not cease,
Thyself to draw me, to push me, and to entreat!

10 (14). [Recitativo. S, T, T, B, B, bc] G min–E maj C

Evangelista
*That disciple was known unto the high priest, and went in with Jesus into the palace of the high priest. But Peter stood at the door without. Then went out that other disciple, which was known unto the high priest, and spake unto her that kept the door, and brought in Peter. Then saith the damsel unto Peter,*

Ancilla
*Art not thou also one of this man's disciples?*
Evangelista
*He saith,*
Petrus
*I am not.*
Evangelista
*And the servants and officers stood there, who had made a fire of coals; for it was cold: and they warmed themselves: and Peter stood with them, and warmed himself. The high priest then asked Jesus of his disciples, and of his doctrine. Jesus answered him,*
Jesus
*I spake openly to the world; I ever taught in the synagogue, and in the temple, whither the Jews always resort; and in secret have I said nothing. Why askest thou me? ask them which heard me, what I have said unto them: behold, they know what I said.*

Evangelista
*And when he had thus spoken, one of the officers which stood by struck Jesus with the palm of his hand, saying,*

Servus
*Solltest du dem Hohenpriester also antworten?*
Evangelista
*Jesus aber antwortete:*
Jesus
*Hab ich übel geredt, so beweise es, daß es böse sei, hab ich aber recht geredt, was schlägest du mich?*

11 (15). CHORAL [S, A, T, B, Bc (+ Instr)] A

**Wer hat dich so geschlagen,**
**Mein Heil, und dich mit Plagen**
**So übel zugericht'?**
**Du bist ja nicht ein Sünder**
**Wie wir und unsre Kinder,**
**Von Missetaten weißt du nicht.**

**Ich, ich und meine Sünden,**
**Die sich wie Körnlein finden**
**Des Sandes an dem Meer,**
**Die haben dir erreget**
**Das Elend, das dich schläget,**
**Und das betrübte Marterheer.**

12[a] (16). [RECITATIVO. T, Bc] fis–E

Evangelista
*Und Hannas sandte ihn gebunden zu dem Hohenpriester Kaiphas. Simon Petrus stund und wärmete sich, da sprachen sie zu ihm:*

12[b] (17). CHORUS [S, A, T, B, Bc (+ Instr)] E

*Bist du nicht seiner Jünger einer?*

12[c] (18). [RECITATIVO. T, T, B, Bc] E–fis

Evangelista
*Er leugnete aber und sprach:*
Petrus
*Ich bins nicht.*
Evangelista
*Spricht des Hohenpriesters Knecht' einer, ein Gefreundter des, dem Petrus das Ohr abgehauen hatte:*

Servus
*Answerest thou the high priest so?*
Evangelista
*Jesus answered him,*
Jesus
*If I have spoken evil, bear witness of the evil: but if well, why smitest thou me?*

11 (15). Chorale [S, A, T, B, bc (+ instr)] A maj C

**What man hath thee thus smitten,**
**My saviour, and with tortures**
**So badly bruised and hurt?**
**For thou art not a sinner,**
**As we are and our children,**
**Thou knowest no transgressions.**

**I, I and my sins,**
**Which are as numerous as small grains**
**Of sand found by the sea,**
**For thee they have brought forth**
**The sorrow, which o'erwhelms thee,**
**And the doleful host of torments.**

12[a] (16). [Recitativo, T, bc] F♯min–E maj C

Evangelista
*Now Annas had sent him bound unto Caiaphas the high priest. And Simon Peter stood and warmed himself. They said therefore unto him,*

12[b] (17). Chorus [S, A, T, B, bc (+ instr)] E maj C

*Art not thou also one of his disciples?*

12[c] (18). [Recitativo. T, T, B, bc] E maj–F♯min C

Evangelista
*He denied it and said,*
Petrus
*I am not.*
Evangelista
*One of the servants of the high priest, being his kinsman whose ear Peter had cut off, saith,*

Servus
*Sahe ich dich nicht im Garten bei ihm?*
Evangelista
*Da verleugnete Petrus abermal, und alsobald krähete der Hahn. Da gedachte Petrus an die Worte Jesu und ging hinaus und weinete bitterlich.*

13 (19). ARIA [T, Str, Bc; Partitur: alle Instr] fis

Ach, mein Sinn,
Wo willt du endlich hin,
Wo soll ich mich erquicken?
Bleib ich hier,
Oder wünsch ich mir
Berg und Hügel auf den Rücken?
Bei der Welt ist gar kein Rat,
Und im Herzen
Stehn die Schmerzen
Meiner Missetat,
Weil der Knecht den Herrn verleugnet hat.

14 (20). CHORAL [S, A, T, B, Bc (+ Instr)] fis–A

**Petrus, der nicht denkt zurück,**
**Seinen Gott verneinet,**
**Der doch auf ein' ernsten Blick**
**Bitterlichen weinet.**
**Jesu, blicke mich auch an,**
**Wenn ich nicht will büßen;**
**Wenn ich Böses hab getan,**
**Rühre mein Gewissen!**

Parte seconda. Nach der Predigt

15 (21). CHORAL [S, A, T, B, Bc (+ Instr)] e

**Christus, der uns selig macht,**
**Kein Bös' hat begangen,**
**Der ward für uns in der Nacht**
**Als ein Dieb gefangen,**

Servus
*Did not I see thee in the garden with him?*
Evangelista
*Peter then denied again: and immediately the cock crew. And Peter remembered the word of Jesus. And he went out, and wept bitterly.*

13 (19). Aria [T, str, bc; Score: all instr] F♯min 3/4

Ah, my soul
Where dost thou wish to go,
Where shall I turn for succour?
Shall I stay,
Or should I wish
Hill and mountain to o'erwhelm me?
In the world there is no counsel,
And in the heart
There stand the pains
Of my transgression,
For the servant hath denied his master.

14 (20). Chorale [S, A, T, B, bc (+ instr)] F♯min–A maj C

**Peter, who doth not think back,**
**And his God denieth,**
**Who yet at a solemn glance**
**Bitter tears doth weep.**
**Jesus, also look on me,**
**When I resist repentance**
**When things evil I have done**
**Stir my inner conscience.**

Parte seconda. After the sermon

15 (21). Chorale [S, A, T, B, bc (+ instr)] E min C

**Christ, the source of our salvation,**
**No evil committed,**
**Who for us was in the night**
**Like a thief arrested,**

**Geführt für gottlose Leut**
**Und fälschlich verklaget,**
**Verlacht, verhöhnt und verspeit,**
**Wie denn die Schrift saget.**

16[a] (22). [Recitativo. T, B, Bc] A–d

Evangelista
*Da führeten sie Jesum von Kaipha vor das Richthaus, und es war frühe. Und sie gingen nicht in das Richthaus, auf daß sie nicht unrein würden, sondern Ostern essen möchten. Da ging Pilatus zu ihnen heraus und sprach:*
Pilatus
*Was bringet ihr für Klage wider diesen Menschen?*
Evangelista
*Sie antworteten und sprachen zu ihm:*

16[b] (23). Chorus [S, A, T, B, Bc (+ Instr)] d

*Wäre dieser nicht ein Übeltäter, wir hätten dir ihn nicht überantwortet.*

16[c] (24). [Recitativo. T, B, Bc] d–a

Evangelista
*Da sprach Pilatus zu ihnen:*
Pilatus
*So nehmet ihr ihn hin und richtet ihn*
*nach eurem Gesetze!*
Evangelista
*Da sprachen die Jüden zu ihm:*

16[d] (25). Chorus [S, A, T, B; Fltr I + II + V I; Bc (+ übrige Instr)] a

*Wir dürfen niemand töten.*

16[e] (26). [Recitativo. T, B, B, Bc] a–a

Evangelista
*Auf daß erfüllet würde das Wort Jesu, welches er sagte,*

**Brought up before godless men**
**And falsely accused,**
**Derided, mocked and spat upon,**
**As the scriptures tell us.**

16[a] (22). [RECITATIVO. T, B, bc] E maj–D min C

Evangelista
*Then led they Jesus from Caiaphas unto the hall of judgment: and it was early; and they themselves went not into the judgment hall, lest they should be defiled; but that they might eat the passover. Pilate then went out unto them, and said,*
Pilatus
*What accusation bring ye against this man?*
Evangelista
*They answered and said unto him,*

16[b] (23). CHORUS [S, A, T, B, bc (+ instr)] D min C

*If he were not a malefactor, we would not have delivered him up unto thee.*

16[c] (24). [RECITATIVO. T, B, bc] D min–A min C

Evangelista
*Then said Pilate unto them,*
Pilatus
*Take ye him, and judge him according to your law.*

Evangelista
*The Jews therefore said unto him,*

16[d] (25). CHORUS [S, A, T, B; fltr I + II + vn I; bc (+ other instr)] A min C

*It is not lawful for us to put any man to death:*

16[e] (26). [RECITATIVO, T, B, B, bc] A min–A min C

Evangelista
*That the saying of Jesus might be fulfilled, which he*

*da er deutete, welches Todes er sterben würde. Da ging Pilatus wieder hinein in das Richthaus und rief Jesu und sprach zu ihm:*

Pilatus

*Bist du der Jüden König?*

Evangelista

*Jesus antwortete:*

Jesus

*Redest du das von dir selbst, oder habens dir andere von mir gesagt?*

Evangelista

*Pilatus antwortete:*

Pilatus

*Bin ich ein Jüde? Dein Volk und die Hohenpriester haben dich mir überantwortet; was hast du getan?*

Evangelista

*Jesus antwortete:*

Jesus

*Mein Reich ist nicht von dieser Welt; wäre mein Reich von dieser Welt, meine Diener würden darob kämpfen, daß ich den Jüden nicht überantwortet würde; aber nun ist mein Reich nicht von dannen.*

17 (27). Choral [S, A, T, B, Bc (+ Instr)] a

**Ach großer König, groß zu allen Zeiten,**
**Wie kann ich gnugsam diese Treu ausbreiten?**
**Keins Menschen Herze mag indes ausdenken,**
**Was dir zu schenken.**

**Ich kanns mit meinen Sinnen nicht erreichen,**
**Womit doch dein Erbarmen zu vergleichen.**
**Wie kann ich dir denn deine Liebestaten**
**Im Werk erstatten?**

18[a] (28). [Recitativo. T, B, B, Bc] F–d

Evangelista

*Da sprach Pilatus zu ihm:*

Pilatus

*So bist du dennoch ein König?*

*spake, signifying what death he should die. Then Pilate entered into the judgment hall again, and called Jesus, and said unto him,*
Pilatus
*Art thou the King of the Jews?*
Evangelista
*Jesus answered him,*
Jesus
*Sayest thou this thing of thyself, or did others tell it thee of me?*
Evangelista
*Pilate answered,*
Pilatus
*Am I a Jew? Thine own nation and the chief priests have delivered thee unto me: what hast thou done?*
Evangelista
*Jesus answered,*
Jesus
*My kingdom is not of this world: if my kingdom were of this world, then would my servants fight, that I should not be delivered to the Jews: but now is my kingdom not from hence.*

17 (27). CHORALE [S, A, T, B, bc (+ instr)] A min C

**Ah mighty King, great in all times and ages,**
**How can I rightly praise this great devotion?**
**No human heart can yet imagine ever,**
**What it may give thee.**

**I cannot with my senses reach and utter**
**With what and how thy mercy to compare.**
**How can I then thy deeds of loving-kindness,**
**In work repay thee?**

18[a] (28). [RECITATIVO. T, B, B, bc] F maj–D min C

Evangelista
*Pilate therefore said unto him,*
Pilatus
*Art thou a king then?*

Evangelista
*Jesus antwortete:*
Jesus
*Du sagsts, ich bin ein König. Ich bin dazu geboren und in die Welt kommen, daß ich die Wahrheit zeugen soll. Wer aus der Wahrheit ist, der höret meine Stimme.*
Evangelista
*Spricht Pilatus zu ihm:*
Pilatus
*Was ist Wahrheit?*
Evangelista
*Und da er das gesaget, ging er wieder hinaus zu den Jüden und spricht zu ihnen:*
Pilatus
*Ich finde keine Schuld an ihm. Ihr habt aber eine Gewohnheit, daß ich euch einen losgebe; wollt ihr nun, daß ich euch der Jüden König losgebe?*
Evangelista
*Da schrieen sie wieder allesamt und sprachen:*

18b (29). CHORUS [S, A, T, B; Hbl + V I in unisono; Bc (+ übrige Instr)] d

*Nicht diesen, sondern Barrabam!*

18c (30). [RECITATIVO. T, Bc] g–g

Evangelista
*Barrabas aber war ein Mörder. Da nahm Pilatus Jesum und geißelte ihn.*

19 (31). ARIOSO [B, Va d'am I, II (o V I, II soli con sordini), Liuto (o Org o Cemb), Bc] Es

Betrachte, meine Seel, mit ängstlichem Vergnügen,
Mit bittrer Lust und halb beklemmtem Herzen
Dein höchstes Gut in Jesu Schmerzen,
Wie dir auf Dornen, so ihn stechen,
Die Himmelsschlüsselblumen blühn!

Evangelista
*Jesus answered,*
Jesus
*Thou sayest that I am a king. To this end was I born, and for this cause came I into the world, that I should bear witness unto the truth. Every one that is of the truth heareth my voice.*
Evangelista
*Pilate saith unto him,*
Pilatus
*What is truth?*
Evangelista
*And when he had said this, he went out again unto the Jews, and saith unto them,*
Pilatus
*I find in him no fault at all. But ye have a custom, that I should release unto you one [at the passover]: will ye therefore that I release unto you the King of the Jews?*
Evangelista
*Then cried they all again, saying,*

18[b] (29). CHORUS [S, A, T, B; ww + vn I in unisono; bc (+ other instr)] D min C

*Not this man, but Barabbas.*

18[c] (30). [RECITATIVO. T, bc] G min–G min C

Evangelista
*Now Barabbas was a robber [murderer]. Then Pilate therefore took Jesus, and scourged him.*

19 (31). ARIOSO [B, va d'am I, II (or vn I, II soli con sordini), liuto (or org or cemb), bc] E♭ maj C

Behold then, o my soul, with timorous pleasure,
With bitter joy and sad and heavy heart,
Thy greatest good in Jesus' sufferings,
How on the thorns, the which do pierce him,
Heaven's primroses flower for thee!

Du kannst viel süße Frucht von seiner Wermut
brechen,
Drum sieh ohn Unterlaß auf ihn!

20 (32). ARIA [T, Va d'am I, II (o V I, II soli con sordini), Bc] c

Erwäge, wie sein blutgefärbter Rücken
In allen Stücken
Dem Himmel gleiche geht,
Daran, nachdem die Wasserwogen
Von unsrer Sündflut sich verzogen,
Der allerschönste Regenbogen
Als Gottes Gnadenzeichen steht!

21[a] (33). [RECITATIVO. T, Bc] g–B

Evangelista
*Und die Kriegsknechte flochten eine Krone von Dornen und satzten sie auf sein Haupt und legten ihm ein Purpurkleid an und sprachen:*

21[b] (34). CHORUS [S, A, T, B, Fltr + Ob I; Fltr + Ob II (Fassung III, IV: + einige V); Bc (+ übrige Instr)] B

*Sei gegrüßet, lieber Jüdenkönig!*

21[c] (35). [RECITATIVO. T, B, Bc] c–g

Evangelista
*Und gaben ihm Backenstreiche. Da ging Pilatus wieder heraus und sprach zu ihnen:*
Pilatus
*Sehet, ich führe ihn heraus zu euch, daß ihr erkennet, daß ich keine Schuld an ihm finde.*
Evangelista
*Also ging Jesus heraus und trug eine Dornenkrone und Purpurkleid. Und er sprach zu ihnen:*
Pilatus
*Sehet, welch ein Mensch!*

Many a sweet fruit thou canst thus from his sorrow
pluck,
Therefore look on him evermore.

20 (32). ARIA [T, va d'am I, II (or vn I, II soli con sordini), bc] C min 12/8

Consider how his back that's stained with blood,
In all its aspects
Like unto the heavens is,
Where, after the watery billows
Of the deluge of our sins have passed,
The most beautiful of rainbows stands
As symbol of the grace of God!

21[a] (33). [RECITATIVO, T, bc] G min–B♭ maj C

Evangelista
*And the soldiers plaited a crown of thorns, and put it on his head, and they put on him a purple robe. And said,*

21[b] (34). CHORUS [S, A, T, B; fltr + ob I; fltr + ob II (Version III, IV: + some vn): bc (+ other instr)] B♭ maj 6/4

*Hail, King of the Jews!*

21[c] (35). [RECITATIVO, T, B, bc] C min–G min C

Evangelista
*And they smote him with their hands. Pilate therefore went forth again, and saith unto them,*
Pilatus
*Behold, I bring him forth to you, that ye may know that I find no fault in him.*
Evangelista
*Then came Jesus forth, wearing the crown of thorns, and the purple robe. And Pilate saith unto them,*
Pilatus
*Behold the man!*

Evangelista
*Da ihn die Hohenpriester und die Diener sahen, schrieen sie und sprachen:*

21[d] (36). CHORUS [S, A, T, B, Str, Bc (Hbl)] g

*Kreuzige, kreuzige!*

21[e] (37). [RECITATIVO. T, B, Bc] g–F

Evangelista
*Pilatus sprach zu ihnen:*
Pilatus
*Nehmet ihr ihn hin und kreuziget ihn; denn ich finde keine Schuld an ihm!*
Evangelista
*Die Jüden antworteten ihm:*

21[f] (38). CHORUS [S, A, T, B, Bc (+ Instr)] F–d

*Wir haben ein Gesetz, und nach dem Gesetz soll er sterben; denn er hat sich selbst zu Gottes Sohn gemacht.*

21[g] (39). [RECITATIVO. T, B, B, Bc] d–E

Evangelista
*Da Pilatus das Wort hörete, fürchtet' er sich noch mehr und ging wieder hinein in das Richthaus und spricht zu Jesu:*
Pilatus
*Von wannen bist du?*
Evangelista
*Aber Jesus gab ihm keine Antwort. Da sprach Pilatus zu ihm:*
Pilatus
*Redest du nicht mit mir? Weißest du nicht, daß ich Macht habe, dich zu kreuzigen, und Macht habe, dich loszugeben?*
Evangelista
*Jesus antwortete:*
Jesus
*Du hättest keine Macht über mich, wenn sie dir nicht*

Evangelista
*When the chief priests therefore and officers saw him, they cried out, saying,*

21[d] (36). Chorus [S, A, T, B, str, bc (ww)] G min C

*Crucify him, crucify him.*

21[e] (37). [Recitativo. T, B, bc] G min–F maj C

Evangelista
*Pilate saith unto them,*
Pilatus
*Take ye him, and crucify him: for I find no fault in him.*
Evangelista
*The Jews answered him,*

21[f] (38). Chorus [S, A, T, B, bc (+ instr)] F maj–D min C

*We have a law, and by our law he ought to die, because he made himself the Son of God.*

21[g] (39). [Recitativo. T, B, B, bc] D min–E maj C

Evangelista
*When Pilate therefore heard that saying, he was the more afraid; And went again into the judgment hall, and saith unto Jesus,*
Pilatus
*Whence art thou?*
Evangelista
*But Jesus gave him no answer. Then saith Pilate unto him,*
Pilatus
*Speakest thou not unto me? knowest thou not that I have power to crucify thee, and have power to release thee?*
Evangelista
*Jesus answered,*
Jesus
*Thou couldest have no power at all against me, except*

*wäre von oben herab gegeben; darum, der mich dir überantwortet hat, der hat's größ're Sünde.*
Evangelista
*Von dem an trachtete Pilatus, wie er ihn losließe.*

22 (40). Choral [S, A, T, B, Bc (+ Instr)] E

**Durch dein Gefängnis, Gottes Sohn,**
**Muß uns die Freiheit kommen;**
**Dein Kerker ist der Gnadenthron,**
**Die Freistatt aller Frommen;**
**Denn gingst du nicht die Knechtschaft ein,**
**Müßt unsre Knechtschaft ewig sein.**

23[a] (41). [Recitativo. T, Bc] h–h

Evangelista
*Die Jüden aber schrieen und sprachen:*

23[b] (42). Chorus [S, A, T, B, Bc (+ Instr)] E–cis

*Lässest du diesen los, so bist du des Kaisers Freund nicht; denn wer sich zum Könige machet, der ist wider den Kaiser.*

23[c] (43). [Recitativo. T, B, Bc] cis–h

Evangelista
*Da Pilatus das Wort hörete, führete er Jesum heraus und satzte sich auf den Richtstuhl an der Stätte, die da heißet: Hochpflaster, auf Ebräisch aber: Gabbatha. Es war aber der Rüsttag in Ostern um die sechste Stunde, und er spricht zu den Jüden:*
Pilatus
*Sehet, das ist euer König!*
Evangelista
*Sie schrieen aber:*

23[d] (44). Chorus [S, A, T, B, Str, Bc (+ Hbl)] h–fis

*Weg, weg mit dem, kreuzige ihn!*

*it were given thee from above: therefore he that delivered me unto thee hath the greater sin.*
Evangelista
*And from thenceforth Pilate sought to release him:*

22 (40). CHORALE [S, A, T, B, bc (+ instr)] E maj C

**Through this thy prison, Son of God,**
**To us must freedom come.**
**Thy dungeon is the throne of grace,**
**The refuge of the faithful.**
**And if thou wast not thus in thrall**
**Our thraldom would eternal be.**

23[a] (41). [RECITATIVO. T, bc] B min–B min C

Evangelista
*But the Jews cried out, saying,*

23[b] (42). CHORUS [S, A, T, B, bc (+ instr)] E min–C♯min C

*If thou let this man go, thou art not Cæsar's friend: whosoever maketh himself a king speaketh against Cæsar.*

23[c] (43). [RECITATIVO, T, B, bc] C♯min–B min C

Evangelista
*When Pilate therefore heard that saying, he brought Jesus forth, and sat down in the judgment seat in a place that is called the Pavement, but in Hebrew, Gabbatha. And it was the preparation of the passover, and about the sixth hour: and he saith unto the Jews,*
Pilatus
*Behold your King!*
Evangelista
*But they cried out,*

23[d] (44). CHORUS [S, A, T, B, str, bc (+ ww)] B min–F♯min C

*Away with him, away with him, crucify him.*

23[e] (45). [RECITATIVO. T, B, Bc] h–h

Evangelista
*Spricht Pilatus zu ihnen:*
Pilatus
*Soll ich euren König kreuzigen?*
Evangelista
*Die Hohenpriester antworteten:*

23[f] (46). CHORUS [S, A, T, B; Fltr I + II; Str + Ob, Ob d'am; Bc] h

*Wir haben keinen König denn den Kaiser.*

23[g] (47). [RECITATIVO. T, Bc] h–g

Evangelista
*Da überantwortete er ihn, daß er gekreuziget würde. Sie nahmen aber Jesum und führeten ihn hin. Und er trug sein Kreuz und ging hinaus zur Stätte, die da heißet Schädelstätt, welche heißet auf Ebräisch: Golgatha.*

24 (48). ARIA ([B solo; S, A, T, Str, Bc] g

Eilt, ihr angefochtnen Seelen,
Geht aus euren Marterhöhlen,
Eilt—Wohin?—nach Golgatha!
  Nehmet an des Glaubens Flügel,
  Flieht—Wohin?—zum Kreuzeshügel,
  Eure Wohlfahrt blüht allda!

25[a] (49). [RECITATIVO. T, Bc] F–B

Evangelista
*Allda kreuzigten sie ihn, und mit ihm zween andere zu beiden Seiten, Jesum aber mitten inne. Pilatus aber schrieb eine Überschrift und satzte sie auf das Kreuz, und war geschrieben: »Jesus von Nazareth, der Jüden König.« Diese Überschrift lasen viel Jüden, denn die Stätte war nahe bei der Stadt, da Jesus gekreuziget ist.*

23[e] (45). [RECITATIVO. T, B, Bc] B min–B min C

Evangelista
*Pilate saith unto them,*
Pilatus
*Shall I crucify your King?*
Evangelista
*The chief priests answered,*

23[f] (46). CHORUS [S, A, T, B; fltr I + II; str + ob, ob d'am; bc] B min C

*We have no king but Cæsar.*

23[g] (47). [RECITATIVO. T, bc] B min–G min C

Evangelista
*Then delivered he him therefore unto them to be crucified. And they took Jesus, and led him away. And he bearing his cross went forth into a place called the place of a skull, which is called in the Hebrew Golgotha:*

24 (48). ARIA [B solo; S, A, T, str, bc] G min 3/8

Hasten, ye souls that are tempted,
Leave your dens of torment,
Hasten—where to?—to Golgotha!
  Take up the wings of faith,
  Flee—Where to?—to the hill of the cross,
  There where your salvation lies.

25[a] (49). [RECITATIVO. T, bc] F maj–B♭ maj C

Evangelista
*Where they crucified him, and two other with him, on either side one, and Jesus in the midst. And Pilate wrote a title, and put it on the cross. And the writing was, JESUS OF NAZARETH THE KING OF THE JEWS. This title then read many of the Jews: for the place where Jesus was crucified was nigh to the city: and it*

*Und es war geschrieben auf ebräische, griechische und lateinische Sprache. Da sprachen die Hohenpriester der Jüden zu Pilato:*

25[b] (50). CHORUS [wie 21[b] (siehe oben)] B

*Schreibe nicht: der Jüden König, sondern daß er gesaget habe: Ich bin der Jüden König.*

25[c] (51). [RECITATIVO. T, B, Bc] B–B

Evangelista
*Pilatus antwortet:*
Pilatus
*Was ich geschrieben habe, das habe ich geschrieben.*

26 (52). CHORAL [S, A, T, B, Bc (+ Instr)] Es

**In meines Herzens Grunde**
**Dein Nam und Kreuz allein**
**Funkelt all Zeit und Stunde,**
**Drauf kann ich fröhlich sein.**
**Erschein mir in dem Bilde**
**Zu Trost in meiner Not,**
**Wie du, Herr Christ, so milde**
**Dich hast geblut' zu Tod!**

27[a] (53). [RECITATIVO. T, Bc] B–C

Evangelista
*Die Kriegsknechte aber, da sie Jesum gekreuziget hatten, nahmen seine Kleider und machten vier Teile, einem jeglichen Kriegesknechte sein Teil, dazu auch den Rock. Der Rock aber war ungenähet, von oben an gewürket durch und durch. Da sprachen sie untereinander:*

27[b] (54). CHORUS [S, A, T, B; Bc geteilt (+ Instr)] C

*Lasset uns den nicht zerteilen, sondern*
*darum losen, wes er sein soll!*

*was written in Hebrew, and Greek, and Latin. Then said the chief priests of the Jews to Pilate,*

25[b] (50). CHORUS [as 21[b] (see above)] B♭ maj 6/4

*Write not, The King of the Jews; but that he said, I am King of the Jews.*

25[c] (51). [RECITATIVO. T, B, bc] B♭ maj–B♭ maj C

Evangelista
*Pilate answered,*
Pilatus
*What I have written I have written.*

26 (52). CHORALE [S, A, T, B, bc (+ instr)] E♭ maj C

**In the recesses of my heart**
**Thy name and cross alone**
**Gleam at all times and hours,**
**Wherefore I can rejoice.**
**Come to me in this image**
**As comfort in my distress,**
**How thou, Lord Christ, so gently**
**Thyself didst bleed to death.**

27[a] (53). [RECITATIVO, T, bc] B♭ maj–C maj C

Evangelista
*Then the soldiers, when they had crucified Jesus, took his garments, and made four parts, to every soldier a part; and also his coat: now the coat was without seam, woven from the top throughout. They said therefore among themselves,*

27[b] (54). CHORUS [S, A, T, B; bc divided (+ instr)] C maj 3/4

*Let us not rend it, but cast lots for it, whose it shall be:*

27ᶜ (55). [Recitativo. T, B, Bc] a–a

Evangelista
*Auf daß erfüllet würde die Schrift, die da saget: »Sie haben meine Kleider unter sich geteilet und haben über meinen Rock das Los geworfen.« Solches taten die Kriegesknechte. Es stund aber bei dem Kreuze Jesu seine Mutter und seiner Mutter Schwester, Maria, Kleophas Weib, und Maria Magdalena. Da nun Jesus seine Mutter sahe und den Jünger dabei stehen, den er lieb hatte, spricht er zu seiner Mutter:*
Jesus
*Weib, siehe, das ist dein Sohn!*
Evangelista
*Darnach spricht er zu dem Jünger:*
Jesus
*Siehe, das ist deine Mutter!*

28 (56). Choral [S, A, T, B, Bc (+ Instr)] A

**Er nahm alles wohl in acht**
**In der letzten Stunde,**
**Seine Mutter noch bedacht,**
**Setzt ihr ein' Vormunde.**
**O Mensch, mache Richtigkeit,**
**Gott und Menschen liebe,**
**Stirb darauf ohn alles Leid,**
**Und dich nicht betrübe!**

29 (57). [Recitativo. T, B, Bc] A–fis

Evangelista
*Und von Stund an nahm sie der Jünger zu sich. Darnach, als Jesus wußte, daß schon alles vollbracht war, daß die Schrift erfüllet würde, spricht er:*

Jesus
*Mich dürstet!*
Evangelista
*Da stund ein Gefäße voll Essigs. Sie fülleten aber einen Schwamm mit Essig und legten ihn um einen Isopen,*

27[c] (55). [RECITATIVO. T, B, bc] A min–A min C

Evangelista
*That the scripture might be fulfilled, which saith, They parted my raiment among them, and for my vesture they did cast lots. These things therefore the soldiers did. Now there stood by the cross of Jesus his mother, and his mother's sister, Mary the wife of Cleophas, and Mary Magdalene. When Jesus therefore saw his mother, and the disciple standing by, whom he loved, he saith unto his mother,*
Jesus
*Woman, behold thy son!*
Evangelista
*Then saith he to the disciple,*
Jesus
*Behold thy mother!*

28 (56). CHORALE [S, A, T, B, bc (+ instr)] A maj C

**He took care of everything,**
**Even at the last hour,**
**Of his mother he did think,**
**And gave her a guardian.**
**O man, strive for what is right,**
**Love both God and human kind,**
**Die thereafter without pain,**
**And do not be sorrowful.**

29 (57). [RECITATIVO. T, B, bc] A maj–F♯min C

Evangelista
*And from that hour that disciple took her unto his own home. After this, Jesus knowing that all things were now accomplished, that the scripture might be fulfilled, saith,*
Jesus
*I thirst.*
Evangelista
*Now there was set a vessel full of vinegar: and they filled a sponge with vinegar, and put it upon hyssop,*

*und hielten es ihm dar zum Munde. Da nun Jesus den*
*Essig genommen hatte, sprach er:*
Jesus
*Es ist vollbracht!*

30 (58). ARIA [A, Str, Va da g sola, Bc] h

Es ist vollbracht!
O Trost vor die gekränkten Seelen!
Die Trauernacht
Läßt nun die letzte Stunde zählen.
Der Held aus Juda siegt mit Macht
Und schließt den Kampf.
Es ist vollbracht!

31 (59). [RECITATIVO. T, Bc] h–fis

Evangelista
*Und neiget das Haupt und verschied.*

32 (60). ARIA [B solo; S, A, T, B (+ Str); Bc] D

Mein teurer Heiland, laß dich fragen,
**Jesu, der du warest tot,**
Da du nunmehr ans Kreuz geschlagen
Und selbst gesagt: Es ist vollbracht,
**Lebest nun ohn Ende,**
Bin ich vom Sterben frei gemacht?
**In der letzten Todesnot**
**Nirgend mich hinwende**
Kann ich durch deine Pein und Sterben
Das Himmelreich ererben?
Ist aller Welt Erlösung da?
**Als zu dir, der mich versühnt,**
**O du lieber Herre!**
Du kannst vor Schmerzen zwar nichts sagen;
**Gib mir nur, was du verdient,**
Doch neigest du das Haupt
Und sprichst stillschweigend: ja.
**Mehr ich nicht begehre!**

*and put it to his mouth. When Jesus therefore had received the vinegar, he said,*
Jesus
*It is finished.*

30 (58). Aria [A, str, va da g sola, bc] B min C

It is finished!
O comfort for afflicted souls!
The night of mourning
Now doth toll the final hour.
With might the hero of Judah triumphs
And ends the strife.
It is finished!

31 (59). [Recitativo, T, bc] B min–F♯min C

Evangelista
*And he bowed his head, and gave up the ghost.*

32 (60). Aria [B solo; S, A, T, B (+ str): bc] D maj 12/8

My dearest saviour, may I ask thee
**Jesus, thou who wast dead,**
Now that thou art nailed to the cross
And thyself hast said: it is finished,
**Thou livest now forever,**
Have I been released from death?
**Nowhere in death's final hour**
**Shall I turn for succour**
Can I through thy pains and death
Heaven now inherit?
Has all the world's salvation come?
**But to thee, who dost redeem me,**
**O thou dearest lord!**
Though nothing thou canst say for pain,
**Give me but what is thy due,**
Yet dost thou bow thy head
And in silence utter: yes.
**More I do not hope for!**

33 (61). [RECITATIVO. T, Bc] e–e

Evangelista

*Und siehe da, der Vorhang im Tempel zerriß in zwei Stück von oben an bis unten aus. Und die Erde erbebete, und die Felsen zerrissen, und die Gräber täten sich auf, und stunden auf viel Leiber der Heiligen.*

34 (62). ARIOSO [T, Fltr I, II; Ob da c I, II (o Ob d'am I, II); Str, Bc] G–C

Mein Herz, indem die ganze Welt
Bei Jesu Leiden gleichfalls leidet,
Die Sonne sich in Trauer kleidet,
Der Vorhang reißt, der Fels zerfällt,
Die Erde bebt, die Gräber spalten,
Weil sie den Schöpfer sehn erkalten,
Was willst du deines Ortes tun?

35 (63). ARIA [S; Fltr I (o I + II o + V I con sordino); Ob da c I (o I + II); Bc] f

Zerfließe, mein Herze, in Fluten der Zähren
Dem Höchsten zu Ehren!
  Erzähle der Welt und dem Himmel die Not:
  Dein Jesus ist tot!

36 (64). [RECITATIVO. T, Bc] c–B

Evangelista

*Die Jüden aber, dieweil es der Rüsttag war, daß nicht die Leichname am Kreuze blieben den Sabbat über (denn desselbigen Sabbats Tag war sehr groß), baten sie Pilatum, daß ihre Beine gebrochen und sie abgenommen würden. Da kamen die Kriegsknechte und brachen dem ersten die Beine und dem andern, der mit ihm gekreuziget war. Als sie aber zu Jesu kamen, da sie sahen, daß er schon gestorben war, brachen sie ihm die Beine nicht; sondern der Kriegsknechte einer eröffnete seine Seite mit einem Speer, und alsobald ging Blut und Wasser heraus. Und der das gesehen hat, der hat es bezeuget, und sein Zeugnis ist*

33 (61). [RECITATIVO. T, bc] E min–E min C

Evangelista
*And, behold, the veil of the temple was rent in twain from the top to the bottom; and the earth did quake, and the rocks rent; And the graves were opened; and many bodies of the saints which slept arose.*

34 (62). ARIOSO [T, fltr I, II; ob da c I, II (or ob d'am I, II); str, bc] G maj–C maj C

My heart, while the whole world
With Jesus' sufferings also suffers,
The sun apparelled is in mourning,
The veil is rent, the rocks crash down,
The earth doth quake, and graves do open,
Because they see their maker die,
What for thy part canst thou do now?

35 (63). ARIA [S; fltr I (or I + II or + vn I con sordino); ob da c I (or I + II); bc] F min 3/8

Dissolve, my heart, in floods of tears
In honour of the highest!
Tell to the world and to heaven your sorrow,
Thy Jesus is dead!

36 (64). [RECITATIVO. T, bc] C min–B♭ maj C

Evangelista
*The Jews therefore, because it was the preparation, that the bodies should not remain upon the cross on the sabbath day (for that sabbath day was an high day), besought Pilate that their legs might be broken, and that they might be taken away. Then came the soldiers, and brake the legs of the first, and of the other which was crucified with him. But when they came to Jesus, and saw that he was dead already, they brake not his legs: But one of the soldiers with a spear pierced his side, and forthwith came there out blood and water. And he that saw it bare record, and his record is true: and he knoweth that he saith true, that ye might*

*wahr, und derselbige weiß, daß er die Wahrheit saget, auf daß ihr gläubet. Denn solches ist geschehen, auf daß die Schrift erfüllet würde: »Ihr sollet ihm kein Bein zerbrechen.« Und abermal spricht eine andere Schrift: »Sie werden sehen, in welchen sie gestochen haben.«*

37 (65). Choral [S, A, T, B, Bc (+ Instr)] f

**O hilf, Christe, Gottes Sohn,**
**Durch dein bitter Leiden,**
**Daß wir dir stets untertan**
**All Untugend meiden,**
**Deinen Tod und sein Ursach**
**Fruchtbarlich bedenken,**
**Dafür, wiewohl arm und schwach,**
**Dir Dankopfer schenken!**

38 (66). [Recitativo. T, Bc] b–c

Evangelista
*Darnach bat Pilatum Joseph von Arimathia, der ein Jünger Jesu war (doch heimlich aus Furcht vor den Jüden), daß er möchte abnehmen den Leichnam Jesu. Und Pilatus erlaubete es. Derowegen kam er und nahm den Leichnam Jesu herab. Es kam aber auch Nikodemus, der vormals bei der Nacht zu Jesu kommen war, und brachte Myrrhen und Aloen untereinander, bei hundert Pfunden. Da nahmen sie den Leichnam Jesu und bunden ihn in leinen Tücher mit Spezereien, wie die Jüden pflegen zu begraben. Es war aber an der Stätte, da er gekreuziget ward, ein Garte, und im Garten ein neu Grab, in welches niemand je geleget war. Daselbst hin legten sie Jesum, um des Rüsttags willen der Jüden, dieweil das Grab nahe war.*

39 (67). Chorus [S, A, T, B; Hbl + V I in unisono; V II, Va, Bc] c

Ruht wohl, ihr heiligen Gebeine,
Die ich nun weiter nicht beweine,
Ruht wohl und bringt auch mich zur Ruh!

*believe. For these things were done, that the scripture should be fulfilled, A bone of him shall not be broken. And again another scripture saith, They shall look on him whom they pierced.*

37 (65). CHORALE [S, A, T, B, bc (+ instr)] F min C

**Help us, Christ, the Son of God,**
**Through thy most bitter pains,**
**To obey thee always,**
**To eschew all evil,**
**Thy death and its cause**
**Fruitfully to ponder,**
**And thus, though poor and weak,**
**To give thankofferings to thee!**

38 (66). [RECITATIVO. T, bc] B♭ min–C min C

Evangelista
*And after this Joseph of Arimathæa, being a disciple of Jesus, but secretly for fear of the Jews, besought Pilate that he might take away the body of Jesus: and Pilate gave him leave. He came therefore, and took the body of Jesus. And there came also Nicodemus, which at the first came to Jesus by night, and brought a mixture of myrrh and aloes, about an hundred pound weight. Then took they the body of Jesus, and wound it in linen clothes with the spices, as the manner of the Jews is to bury. Now in the place where he was crucified there was a garden; and in the garden a new sepulchre, wherein was never man yet laid. There laid they Jesus therefore because of the Jews' preparation day; for the sepulchre was nigh at hand.*

39 (67). CHORUS [S, A, T, B; ww + vn I in unisono; vn II, va, bc] C min 3/4

Sleep well, ye holy relics,
Which I no longer now bewail,
Sleep well and also bring me sleep!

Das Grab, so euch bestimmet ist
Und ferner keine Not umschließt,
Macht mir den Himmel auf und schließt die Holle
zu.

40 (68). CHORAL [S, A, T, B, Bc (+ Instr)] Es

**Ach Herr, laß dein lieb Engelein**
**Am letzten End die Seele mein**
**In Abrahams Schoß tragen,**
**Den Leib in seim Schlafkämmerlein**
**Gar sanft ohn einge Qual und Pein**
**Ruhn bis am jüngsten Tage!**
**Alsdenn vom Tod erwecke mich,**
**Daß meine Augen sehen dich**
**In aller Freud, o Gottes Sohn,**
**Mein Heiland und Genadenthron!**
**Herr Jesu Christ, erhöre mich,**
**Ich will dich preisen ewiglich!**

Anhang

Die nur zu Fassung II gehörigen Sätze

I[II]. CHORAL [S, A, T, B, Fltr I, II, Ob I, II, Str, Bc] Es

**O Mensch, bewein dein Sünde groß,**
**Darum Christus seins Vaters Schoß**
**Äußert und kam auf Erden;**
**Von einer Jungfrau rein und zart**
**Für uns er hie geboren ward,**
**Er wollt der Mittler werden.**
**Den Toten er das Leben gab**
**Und legt dabei all Krankheit ab**
**Bis sich die Zeit herdrange,**
**Daß er für uns geopfert würd,**
**Trüg unser Sünden schwere Bürd**
**Wohl an dem Kreuze lange.**

The grave, which is your destined place
And now no sorrow knows,
Doth open heaven up for me and shuts the gates
of hell.

40 (68). CHORALE [S, A, T, B, bc (+ instr)] E♭ maj C

**O Lord, let thy dear angel small**
**At the last hour translate my soul**
**To the bosom of Abraham,**
**The body in its small place of rest**
**Lie gently without hurt and pain**
**Resting until judgment day!**
**And then awake me from the dead,**
**That with mine eyes I shall see thee**
**In joy eternal, Son of God,**
**My saviour and the throne of grace!**
**Lord Jesus Christ, o hear my cry,**
**I wish to praise thee eternally!**

Appendix

Movements only in Version II

I[1]. CHORALE [S, A, T, B, fltr I, II, ob I, II, str, bc] E♭ maj C

**O man, bewail thy sin so great,**
**For which Christ his father's bosom**
**Left and came down to earth;**
**Of a virgin pure and tender**
**He here below for us was born,**
**To be our mediator.**
**The dead he did restore to life,**
**And every illness he did cure,**
**Until at last the hour was come**
**When he for us was sacrificed,**
**The heavy burden of our sins**
**To bear so long upon the cross.**

11[+]. Aria [B (solo), S (Choral), Fltr I, II, Bc] fis

Himmel reiße, Welt erhebe,
Fallt in meinen Trauerton,
**Jesu, deine Passion**
Sehet meine Qual und Angst,
Was ich, Jesu, mit dir leide!
**Ist mir lauter Freude,**
Ja, ich zähle deine Schmerzen,
O zerschlagner Gottessohn,
**Deine Wunden, Kron und Hohn**
Ich erwähle Golgatha
Vor dies schnöde Weltgebäude.
**Meines Herzens Weide.**
Werden auf den Kreuzeswegen
Deine Dornen ausgesät,
**Meine Seel auf Rosen geht,**
Weil ich in Zufriedenheit
Mich in deine Wunden senke,
**Wenn ich dran gedenke,**
So erblick ich in dem Sterben,
Wenn ein stürmend Wetter weht,
**In dem Himmel eine Stätt**
Diesen Ort, dahin ich mich
Täglich durch den Glauben lenke.
**Mir deswegen schenke!**

13[II]. Aria [T, Str, Bc] A

Zerschmettert mich, ihr Felsen und ihr Hügel,
Wirf, Himmel, deinen Strahl auf mich!
Wie freventlich, wie sündlich, wie vermessen
Hab ich, o Jesu, dein vergessen!
Ja, nähm ich gleich der Morgenröte Flügel,
So holte mich mein strenger Richter wieder;
Ach! fallt vor ihm in bittern Tränen nieder!

19[II]. Aria [T, Ob I, II, Bc] C

Ach windet euch nicht so, geplagte Seelen,
Bei eurer Kreuzesangst und Qual!

II[+]. Aria [B (solo), S (chorale), fltr I, II, bc] F♯min C

Heavens open, o world rise up
Join me in my mourning strain,
**Jesus, thy very passion**
See my torments and my fear,
That with thee I suffer, Jesus!
**Is my delight and joy,**
Yes, I count thy sufferings,
Bruised and battered Son of God,
**Thy wounds, thy crown and thy derision**
I have chosen Golgotha
Not the baseness of the world.
**Are the pastures of my heart.**
If on the stations of the cross
Thy thorns are strewn and scattered,
**My soul on roses walks,**
Because I with contentment
Sink myself into thy wounds,
**When I remember it,**
Thus I perceive in dying,
In stormy times and weather,
**A place above in heaven,**
This place, to which I turn
And daily strive by means of faith.
**For this reason grant me!**

13[I]. Aria [T, str, bc] A maj C

Break me asunder, ye rocks and ye hills,
Cast, heaven, down on me thy bolt!
How impious, how sinful, how presumptuous
That I, Jesus, have forgotten thee!
Yea, were I to take the wings of dawn,
My stern judge would bring me back;
Ah! with bitter tears sink down before him!

19[I]. Aria [T, ob I, II, Bc] C maj C

Ah, do not writhe thus, tormented souls,
In your torment and terror of the cross!

Könnt ihr die unermeßne Zahl
Der harten Geißelschläge zählen,
So zählet auch die Menge eurer Sünden,
Ihr werdet diese größer finden!

40^II^. CHORAL [S, A, T, B; Fltr + Ob I; Fltr + Ob II; Str, Bc] g

**Christe, du Lamm Gottes,**
**Der du trägst die Sünd' der Welt,**
**Erbarm dich unser!**
**Christe, du Lamm Gottes,**
**Der du trägst die Sünd' der Welt,**
**Erbarm dich unser!**
**Christe, du Lamm Gottes,**
**Der du trägst die Sünd' der Welt,**
**Gib uns dein' Frieden!**
**Amen.**

Die zu Fassung IV geänderten Texte

9^IV^. ARIA [S; Fltr I + II; Bc] B

Ich folge dir gleichfalls, mein Heiland, mit Freuden
Und lasse dich nicht,
Mein Heiland, mein Licht,
Mein sehnlicher Lauf
Hört eher nicht auf,
Bis daß du mich lehrest, geduldig zu leiden.

19^IV^. ARIOSO [B, V I, II soli con sordini, Org o Cemb, Bc] Es

Betrachte, meine Seel, mit ängstlichem
Vergnügen,
Mit bittrer Lust und halb beklemmtem Herzen
Dein höchstes Gut in Jesu Schmerzen.
Sieh hier auf Ruten, die ihn drängen,
Vor deine Schuld den Isop blühn
Und Jesu Blut auf dich zur Reinigung versprengen,
Drum sieh ohn Unterlaß auf ihn!

If you can count the untold number
Of the hard scourging lash's strokes,
Then also count the number of your sins,
And you will find that it is greater!

40[I]. CHORALE [S, A, T, B; fltr + ob I; fltr + ob II; str, bc] G min C

**O Christ, thou Lamb of God**
**That takest away the sins of the world,**
**Have mercy upon us!**

**O Christ, thou Lamb of God,**
**That takest away the sins of the world,**
**Have mercy upon us!**

**O Christ, thou Lamb of God,**
**That takest away the sins of the world,**
**Grant us thy peace!**
**Amen.**

The texts altered in Version IV

9[IV]. ARIA [S; fltr I + II; bc] B♭ maj 3/8

I follow thee also, my saviour, with gladness,
And will not leave thee,
My saviour, my light.
My anxious path
Shall not come to an end,
Until thou hast taught me to suffer with patience.

19[IV]. ARIOSO [B, vn I, II soli con sordini, org or cemb, bc] E♭ maj C

Behold then, o my soul, with timorous
pleasure,
With bitter joy and sad and heavy heart,
Thy greatest good in Jesus' sufferings.
See here the rods, the which do hurt him,
Where for thy guilt the hyssop blooms,
And Jesus' blood on thee for purification sprinkle,
Therefore look on him evermore.

20[IV]. Aria [T, V I, II soli con sordini, Bc] c

Mein Jesu, ach! dein schmerzhaft bitter Leiden
Bringt tausend Freuden,
Es tilgt der Sünden Not.
Ich sehe zwar mit vielen Schrecken
Den heilgen Leib mit Blute decken;
Doch muß mir dies auch Lust erwekken,
Es macht mich frei von Höll und Tod.

Der nachträglich geänderte Text (geplant zu Fassung IV?)

39. Chorus [wie oben zu Satz 39] c

Ruht wohl, ihr heiligen Gebeine,
Um die ich nicht mehr trostlos weine,
Ich weiß, einst gibt der Tod mir Ruh.
Nicht stets umschließet mich die Gruft,
Einst, wenn Gott, mein Erlöser, ruft,
Dann eil auch ich verklärt dem Himmel Gottes zu.

20$^{IV}$. ARIA [T, vn I, II soli con sordini, bc] C min 12/8

My Jesus, ah thy painful bitter suffering
Brings a thousand joys,
It effaces sin and distress.
Although I see with great dismay
The holy body smeared with blood;
Yet this must also give me pleasure,
It sets me free from hell and death.

Text altered at a later date (for inclusion in Version IV?)

39. CHORUS [as above, movement 39] C min 3/4

Sleep well, ye holy relics,
For which disconsolate I weep no more,
I know that death will give me sleep.
Not always shall the grave surround me,
And once, when God, my Saviour, calls,
Then to God's heaven shall I speed transfigured.

# INDEX